Berlitz®
Goa

Text by David Abram
Photography by David Abram
Series Editor: Tony Halliday

Berlitz POCKET GUIDE

Goa

First Edition 2006

PHOTOGRAPHY CREDITS
All pictures by David Abram/Apa, except pages 15 David Abram; 23 AP/Empics; 19 Hans Höfer; 92 Britta Jaschinski; 16, 20, 48, 48 Bill Wassman
Cover photograph: David Wootton/Alamy

CONTACTING THE EDITORS
Every effort has been made to provide accurate information in this publication, but changes are inevitable. The publisher cannot be responsible for any resulting loss, inconvenience or injury. We would appreciate it if readers would call our attention to any errors or outdated information by contacting Berlitz Publishing, PO Box 7910, London SE1 1WE, England. Fax: (44) 20 7403 0290; e-mail: berlitz@apaguide.co.uk www.berlitzpublishing.com

© 2006 Apa Publications GmbH & Co. Verlag KG, Singapore Branch, Singapore

Printed in Singapore by Insight Print Services (Pte) Ltd, 38 Joo Koon Road, Singapore 628990.
Tel: (65) 6865-1600. Fax: (65) 6861-6438

Berlitz Trademark Reg. U.S. Patent Office and other countries. Marca Registrada

Ingo's Night Market (page 56), much cooler than the Anjuna flea market, in every sense

Goa's distinctive Hindu temples cluster around the town of Ponda in central Goa (page 45)

The huge churches of Old Goa (page 36) tower over the palm canopy at the heart of the state

TOP TEN ATTRACTIONS

Elegant old Portuguese-era houses dot the hinterland of south Goa's hub town, Margao (page 63) ▼

Fontainhas, in the capital, Panjim, is lined with colour-washed 19th-century houses (page 32)

◄

Miles of empty beach stretch either side of Benaulim (page 70), in south Goa

►

In the far south, palm-backed Palolem beach (page 73) is a beautiful crescent of golden sand

▼

Terekol Fort (page 62), in the far north, overlooks an empty stretch of sandy coastline

►

Mapusa market, the place to soak up local colour (page 51)

►

Dudhsagar (page 49) is the second-highest waterfall in India

►

CONTENTS

Fact Sheets

INTRODUCTION

Although only a little over 100km (60 miles) from north to south, Goa, India's smallest state, forms one of the most distinctive pieces in the great cultural mosaic of the subcontinent. For more than four-and-a-half centuries it was ruled as a Portuguese colony – the linchpin of a vast trade empire stretching from Japan to Lisbon. As such, its major influences tended to come from across the sea rather than across its borders. Insulated from the rest of coastal India by miles of unnavigable tidal rivers, these influences subsequently took root and blossomed into a culture that was neither entirely Indian nor European, but something in between, with its own unique styles of architecture, cuisine and dress. Along with the idyllic tropical climate and paradise landscape of palm-fringed white-sand beaches, it is this hybrid Indo-Portuguese atmosphere that lends a special complexion to any holiday in Goa.

Valuable Trading Port

Long before the arrival of Europeans, the region now known as Goa, midway down India's fertile southwest coast – the Konkan – thrived as a trading port. Recognising it as a potential base from which to organise his own country's commerce in spices from southeast Asia, the naval commander, Afonso de Albuquerque, stormed the then Muslim stronghold, put its inhabitants to the sword and founded the capital of Portugal's *Estado da India* on the banks of the Mandovi River.

Within a matter of a few years, ships laden with horses, spices, Chinese opium and silks, African slaves, gold and ivory were racing to its harbour. Fortune-seekers and proselytising priests poured in from across the globe on the back

Fishermen mending their nets

of this trade, and a magnificent crop of churches were erected in a city that became known as the 'Rome of the Orient'. But the boom was short-lived. By the end of the 17th century, rival European powers, the Dutch and British, had all but strangled Portuguese trade in the Indies, leaving Goa's population to dwindle from plague and its harbour to clog with silt. By the time of Richard Burton's visit in 1850, the once resplendent capital was a scene of 'utter destitution', its population '…as sepulchral-looking as the spectacle around them'.

Today, with a population of around 1.4 million, Goa is no longer the run-down Lusitanian backwater it was at the time Jawaharlal Nehru sent in the India army to annex the colony in 1961. Mass tourism, fast air and rail connections with Mumbai (Bombay), and mass in-migration from neighbouring Maharasthra (to the north) and Karnataka (to the east and south) are blurring its boundaries. Yet much of what has long distinguished it from the rest of the country – its Indo-Portuguese heritage – still survives.

Christianity, the religion of around one-third of Goans, is perhaps the most visible legacy of colonial rule. Travelling around the palm-shaded villages of the state's heartland, you'll see white-washed churches, garlanded wayside crosses and congregations strolling to Mass in smartly tailored, European-style dresses and suits. In marked contrast with the rest of the country, alcohol enjoys a high profile too, as

> **Cashews and chillies were commodities originally introduced by the Portuguese, which have since become an integral part of local life. After iron ore, cashew nuts are Goa's principal export, while chillies have become an essential ingredient of almost all Goan dishes, including that most hybrid of all local preparations, the sour, fiery sauce known as vindaloo (derived from the Portuguese *vinho* and *alho* – 'wine' and 'garlic').**

Shades of colonial days at this Portuguese-era mansion

it has done since the colony's beginnings. Every hamlet has its bar, and the resorts are crammed with pubs and beach shacks that do a roaring trade in Kingfisher beers and cocktails made of *feni* – a potent concoction distilled from palm sap.

European and Indian Fusions

Portuguese influence is most pronounced in the centre of the state, in and around its main towns: Panjim (the capital), Mapusa (hub of northern Goa), Margao (in the south), and the industrial port of Vasco, just to the west of the airport. However, outside the core of the old colony, in the outlying area known as the *Novas Conquistas* (New Conquests), Hinduism reasserts itself as the predominant faith. The domes and towers of brightly coloured temples, fusing European architectural traits with more traditional Indian motifs, nose above the palm canopy, saris replace dresses and the motorcycles sport images of Ganesh instead of Our Lady. However, the two religions coexist with remarkable ease all over Goa. Hindus and Christians frequently celebrate one another's festivals (sending sweets to their neighbours, for example, at Christmas and *Diwali*), worship at the same shrines (notably that of the state's patron saint, Francis Xavier), and never indulge in the communal violence that afflicts many other regions of India.

This spirit of tolerance in part accounts for the speed with which tourism took root in Goa. When the first hippies colonised the beaches in the 1960s, local fishermen regarded their public nudity, cannabis-smoking and generally strange behaviour with amused detachment, as they did when the first charter flights arrived from the UK two decades later. But few could have guessed the dramatic impact this second wave of Westerners would have on the coastal landscape.

Sosse garde (laid back) is the Portuguese term often used to describe the typically Goan laissez-faire attitude to life;

Beach shack at Aswem

although the phrase puts a somewhat simplistic gloss on what has become a dynamic, fast-developing part of the world, it still has a ring of truth. As a visitor, you'll quickly be seduced by the unhurried pace of the coastal villages. Lounging on the beaches, with the crash of surf drifting through the coconut trees, the rest of the world will soon seem like a distant memory.

The entire 101-km (62-mile) Goan coastline is indented with beautiful beaches, ranging from vast sweeps of sand to tiny coves only accessible by boat. In a fortnight, you could conceivably visit a different one each day, though in practice most visitors stick close to their chosen resorts, so the decision where to stay is important *(see* Which Beach? *on page 12).*

Exploring the State

You'd be missing out on some memorable experiences if you spent your entire trip dozing on the sand. Excursions inland can vary from shopping trips to local towns to expeditions through the tropical forests in the Western Ghat mountains. The most popular day trips in the state are to the Anjuna flea market and Ingo's Night Market, both in northern Goa, which offer a huge range of clothes and Indian souvenirs.

The ruins of the former Portuguese capital at Old Goa and its modern counterpart, Panjim, are the other obvious targets for a day away from the coast. But you might also be tempted by the exotic spice plantations and temples around Ponda, in central Goa, or by the waterfalls of Dudhsagar, in the hills along the Karnatakan border. In addition, the countryside around Margao, in south Goa, holds several stately Goan *palacios* whose aristocratic owners open them for public viewing, particularly the Perreira-Braganza/Menezes-Braganza house in Chandor.

For anyone with enough time to venture beyond the borders of Goa, two very special destinations lie within range of longer forays. A couple of hours by train south down the

Which Beach?

Each of Goa's resorts has its own distinct character, appealing to very different kinds of holidaymakers. **Calangute**, a cluttered and dishevelled town in north Goa strung behind an 11-km (7-mile) strip of sand, is popular mainly with domestic visitors who travel there by bus on day trips from Panjim. At the southern limit of the same beach, **Candolim** is a predominantly British package enclave, overlooked by the former Portuguese stronghold, Fort Aguada.

Younger package tourists gravitate to **Baga**, a resort at the northern end of Calangute beach. Along its busy main drag, signs advertising karaoke nights, 'Full English Breakfasts' and 'Happy Hours' jostle for attention with Kashmiri handicraft vendors and restaurants offering everything from authentic Italian cuisine to cocktails.

Anjuna has always been a bastion of a harder-edged, more hedonistic hippy tourism, with its drug-fuelled full-moon parties and techno dance music, which you can sample at the famous Paradiso Club on the seafront after the flea market.

Beyond the reach of package tourism, **Arambol**, Goa's northernmost village, remains essentially a hang-out for long-staying 'alternative' visitors. If you've come to India to learn yoga, have ayurvedic massages or do t'ai chi on the beach, this is the place for you.

South Goa is on the whole much more sedate than the north, with most visitors corralled inside one of the five-star resorts backing **Colva** beach. Stretching for 25km (15 miles), it remains comparatively uncrowded even in peak season. While the rather run-down resort of Colva itself soaks up most of the domestic tourist traffic, independent travellers tend to congregate in neighbouring **Benaulim** – a mainly Catholic fishing village that has retained plenty of traditional Goan charm. It also offers the best selection of budget guest houses in the area.

In the far south, **Palolem** is undeniably Goa's most picturesque beach: golden sand fringed with coconut palms. Remote and unfrequented until the early 1990s, it's now popular with backpackers.

coast, Gokarna is an important Hindu pilgrimage town that will give you a taste of 'real India', complete with incense- filled temples and sacred beaches. More intense still, the ruins of the medieval capital of Vijayangar, better known as Hampi, provide one of the subcontinent's great spectacles: miles of exquisite ruined temples, palaces and streets, spread below an otherworldly landscape of boulder hills.

Lamani women at Mapusa

With the exception of Gokarna and Hampi, getting to most of these places without your own transport is next to impossible, and most visitors rent a Maruti mini-van taxi and driver for day trips *(see page 123)*.

When to Go

The ideal time to visit Goa is between mid-November, after the last of the monsoon humidity has evaporated, and early March, when the heat starts to build again. Over these relatively cool winter months, maximum temperatures average around 28°C (82°F), and humidity levels are low. You can expect clear skies every day, cool seawater to swim in, and fresh nights. Go any earlier, and you'll have to contend with uncomfortably cloying air and the odd downpour, while from mid-March the days are intensely hot with sticky nights.

A BRIEF HISTORY

When it was finally absorbed into the Republic of India in 1961, Goa was essentially a remote outpost of a long-defunct empire, as physically remote as it was culturally distant from the rest of the subcontinent. But the region wasn't always a forgotten backwater. Centuries before the Portuguese made it the nerve centre of their vast maritime trade empire, the port of Hindu Govapuri on the Zuari River was a thriving capital in its own right, with coffers overflowing from the trade in Arab horses and spices that passed through its busy harbour. Merchants from Persia, the Gulf and East Africa mingled in the city's streets with Muslims and Hindus from across southern India, lending to Goa the far-reaching, culturally mixed roots that have always been its defining trait.

Early History

Echoes of Goa's prehistory resonate through the ancient Sanskrit epic, the *Mahabharata*, which identifies the Konkan region as 'Gopakapattna' – 'Cow Herd Country' – one of the seven sacred territories claimed by the sage Parasurama after he fired an arrow west from the Sayadhri Hills. The sea is said to have receded from the spot where the arrow landed, revealing a land of great natural abundance.

Historians have tended to interpret the myth as a kind of transmission from ancient times, when the Konkan coast was forced upwards by geological upheavals and subsequently cleared by Aryan settlers from the northwest. The incomers brought with them not only knowledge of agriculture, but also the religious traditions of Brahmanical Hinduism.

However, more recent archaeological evidence suggests that Goa was inhabited much earlier than this first wave of in-migration. Rock art discovered in 1993 at Usgalimal and Kajur, in a remote forest district of south Goa, shows hunting and religious images dating from the late Stone Age (10,000–8,000BC), while arrow tips found around the headwaters of the Mandovi, near Dudhsagar waterfalls, have been carbon dated to around 100,000BC.

As part of Aparanta Desh, the area first entered the history books when it formed the far southwestern fringe of the vast Mauryan empire in the 3rd century BC. Ashoka, the militaristic emperor who famously renounced violence and converted to Buddhism, dispatched the missionary monk, Dharmakshita, to promulgate the Buddha's teachings of non-violence, *Dharma* ('the Law'), and small rock-cut cave temples were established at important trade crossroads (several of which survive at isolated spots in the Goan interior).

Usgalimal rock carvings

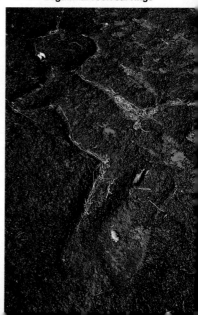

The Hindu Age

The plough and literacy were introduced to the region during the Mauryan era, but the empire faltered when Ashoka died in 231BC. Thereafter, it fell under the sway of a succession of Hindu dynasties who ruled as suzerains from distant capitals, exacting tribute from its local rulers in exchange for protection.

The first truly home-grown Goan dynasty, the Kadambas, emerged at the end of the first

12th-century Ponda carving

millennium, based initially at Chandrapura (Chandor in south Goa) and later Govapuri (or Gopakapattna), at the mouth of the Zuari *(Agnashini)* River. Bolstered by a thriving trade in Arab horses from Hormuz (which were exchanged mainly for Indian calicoes, areca nuts, rice and spices), Kadamba rule saw its golden age under King Jayakeshi II (AD1104–48), whose symbol, the rampant Lion *(Simha lanchana),* still speeds up and down the state highways on the side of government buses. Civic buildings, temples and charitable institutions were founded across the kingdom during his reign. Arab merchants were also encouraged to settle in the capital with grants of land and promises of religious freedom, and contributed much to its prosperity.

Muslim Conquests

A much less benign brand of Islam began to make its presence felt between the 11th and 14th centuries, as Muslim raiders descended from the north in search of plunder. The most devastating incursions were those mounted by the Sultan of Delhi, Ala-uddin-Khilji, whose three vicious attacks reduced Govapuri to ruins.

The following 25 years saw the control of Goa slip from the Muslim Bahmanis, the most powerful Muslim kingdom in the Deccan at that time, to their arch rivals, the Hindu Vijayangars, who took the region in 1378 and established a lasting peace. Under their rule, trade flourished once again through Govapuri, which grew to become the empire's chief port.

The Bahmani counter-attack took nearly a century to materialise. But when it came, the Muslim invasion – a two-pronged assault by land and sea involving 60,000 men-at-arms – reduced the city to a ruinous state from which it would never recover. A new capital, Ela, was founded on the opposite, northern side of the island.

Fuelled as ever by the Arabian horse trade, Ela's rise was given added impetus by Yusuf Adil Shah, the first Sultan of Bijapur. His dynasty was one of the five Muslim kingdoms that arose in the Deccan from the ashes of the Bahmanis, and Bijapur decided to develop Ela as its principal seaport. Impressive mosques, palaces and fortifications were erected in the town in the 1490s, but the Adil Shah's rule would be short-lived.

Near the Church of St Cajetan in Old Goa, a basalt doorframe mounted on a platform stands as a lone survivor from the Adil Shah's palace. It bears distinctly Hindu ornamentation that suggests its architects may themselves have originally plundered the stone from a previous structure.

The *Estado da India*

A new threat to the Konkan region's political and economic security arose at the end of the 15th century with the appearance on Indian shores of the Portuguese. Driven by a quest to find 'Christians and Spices', Vasco da Gama first crossed the Arabian Sea to reach the Malabar Coast of southwest India in 1498. By opening up a direct maritime route to the spiceries of the East Indies, bypassing Turkish, Egyptian and Venetian control of the Red Sea and Mediterranean, the voyage paved the way for potentially vast profits from the spice trade, in particular pepper, prized in Europe as a meat preservative.

First, however, the Portuguese had to exploit their superior naval power and secure control of the Indian Ocean. Strategic ports were duly seized in the Persian Gulf and along the East African coast, and a forced licensing system imposed whereby ships, in exchange for a permit guaranteeing free passage, were obliged to pay duties on their cargoes at customs posts. In addition, a strict monopoly was implemented on pepper and other key commodities.

This proved extraordinarily profitable for the Portuguese. By the start of the 16th century, they were in need of a permanent capital from which to administer their rapidly expanding empire. Goa may never have attracted Portuguese attention at all had not the remnants of a hostile Turkish fleet limped there for a refit after the Battle of Diu in 1509. Afonso de Albuquerque, an ambitious veteran of the North African *reconquista*, was sent by Lisbon to mop up the enemy ships.

Advised by a Vijayangar admiral, Thimmayya, that the port's Bijapuri rulers had left it lightly defended, Albuquerque sailed with his force up the Mandovi and took the city almost unopposed in 1510. However, a massive counter-attack was launched by the Sultan of Bijapur a few months later, forcing the Portuguese back to the river mouth. With their retreat blocked by heavy monsoon seas, the invaders were sitting

Afonso de Albuquerque

ducks for the Muslim cannons, but managed to escape south to Anjediv Island, where they were reinforced by more ships from Portugal. Much to the surprise of the sultan, who had already withdrawn most of his army, Albuquerque straight away waged a second, decisive strike on 24 November 1510 – St Catherine's Day. The Portuguese won control of the city, slaughtering 6,000 of its Muslim inhabitants, in four days.

'Goa Dourada'

Albuquerque immediately set about rebuilding what he'd recognised from the outset would make a perfect capital for the new *Estado da India*. Fair-skinned Muslim women captured in the sacking of the port were given as wives to his soldiers, few of whom had any prospects of ever returning to their homeland.

Trade, merchants, finance, shipwrights, migrant workers and legions of fortune-seekers from across Europe and Asia

Church of St Francis Xavier, Old Goa

soon began pouring in, along with religious orders in search of new converts.

Travellers' accounts of the city at its height, dubbed 'Goa Dourada' or 'Golden Goa', enthused about the amazing wealth of its bazaars and the luxurious lifestyles indulged in by its elite *hidalgos*, or nobility. Everyone, from the viceroy down to humble clergymen, dabbled in illegal private trade and in many cases amassed considerable fortunes.

Installed in elegant *palacios*, Goa's wealthier citizens, whether Portuguese or permanent *mestiço* residents born of mixed marriages in the colony, kept large retinues of black African slaves and led lives whose decadence and profligacy soon started to scandalise the court back home. Liquor, prostitution and adultery were rife, and violent crime a constant menace. The monsoons, when sailing was suspended and the soldiery cast adrift without pay by the state to roam begging in the streets, were a particularly lawless and dangerous time.

To restore some semblance of moral probity, the King of Portugal dispatched the Jesuit Order, under the Basque missionary priest Francis Xavier, to the colony in 1542. His arrival, and that of a new vicar general the same year, signalled the start of a much less tolerant attitude to Hinduism. Temples were destroyed, laws were passed banning worship of icons at home and whole villages forcibly converted.

At the behest of Francis Xavier, the dreaded Holy Office, or Inquisition, also came to Goa to root out heresy, targeting Hindus and the many formerly Jewish 'New Christians' who'd come to the Indies to flee the Inquisition in Iberia. In the 200 years of its operations, more than 16,000 people were murdered or incarcerated in the Inquisition's dungeons.

St Francis Xavier

The man chosen in May 1542 to head the Jesuit mission to the Indies to 'clean up' colonial Goa, was a young Basque priest named Francis Xavier. More than 450 years later, the impact of his stay continues to be felt. Goencho Sahib, as he became known, is still adored by Goan Catholics. By performing miracles such as healing the sick and raising the dead, 'SFX' notched up an unbelievable 30,000 conversions in southern India before his death, in China, in 1552.

Yet Goa's patron saint is perhaps more celebrated for the extraordinary circumstances of his death – or more precisely, the fact his body, when disinterred, proved incorruptible. The news of the miracle caused a sensation, attracting relic-hunters and pilgrims from across the Christian world. These days, Goencho Sahib's wizened corpse looks far from intact, but it still casts a powerful spell over the faithful, who come in their hundreds of thousands every 10 years for the Expositions, when the fabled casket in which it rests is lifted off its pedestal and placed within reach of the public.

> The hedonism that held sway in Goa in the late 16th and 17th centuries is understandable given the extraordinarily low life expectancy of its inhabitants. Hospital records show that half of the city's population perished in the cholera epidemics of 1543 and 1570, while a further 25,000 died from disease in the first three decades of the 1600s.

The Empire in Decline

By the end of the 16th century, Portuguese fortunes in Asia had already started to wane. Repeated epidemics had devastated the population of the capital, while rival European powers, the Dutch and, to a lesser extent, the British, were picking off Lusitanian trading posts from the Moluccas to East Africa. Goa's own harbour was also becoming blocked by silt and inaccessible to ships.

With its trade monopolies compromised and the population of Goa in free fall, Portugal could offer little more than token resistance when the borders of its Indian colony were repeatedly menaced by Bijapuri, Moghul and Maratha armies in the 17th and 18th centuries. Some pride and territory were salvaged during the *Novas Conquistas* (New Conquests) of the 1780s, when the northern- and southernmost districts of Goa were added as a buffer zone against foreign incursion. But the state of the capital itself, substantially dismantled during an abortive plan to relocate it to Mormugao in the 1700s, only worsened. By the 19th century, it was effectively a giant ruin, smothered in jungle and all but deserted.

The viceroy and colonial administration had decamped to a more salubrious site downriver at Panjim; and it was to here that Viceroy Dom Manuel Port'e Castro (1826–35) decided to relocate the capital in the mid-1830s. Paid for by profits from a short-lived boom in the Portuguese opium trade with China, a grid of grand civic buildings sprang up on the newly drained and levelled land near the river mouth.

Liberation

Nevertheless, disenchantment at Portuguese rule grew year by year, particularly among the Hindu majority, who were still treated as second-class citizens, and denied access to government jobs and other positions of influence. A series of minor rebellions were summarily dealt with by the colonial government in the late 19th and early 20th centuries. Goa's newly created, pro-independence press galvanised the fledgling freedom movement after the overthrow of the Portuguese monarchy in 1910. But hopes that the colony would soon be granted independence received a setback in 1932, when the right-wing and pro-colonial António Salazar became Portugal's dictator.

Locals welcome Indian troops following 'Operation Vijay'

Salazar refused to relinquish control of Goa to the newly inaugurated Republic of India in 1947, and somehow managed to convince several world leaders that he was right in doing so. However, Indian Prime Minister Jawaharlal Nehru eventually gave up trying to negotiate and ordered an invasion of Goa. 'Liberation' – or 'Operation Vijay' as it was dubbed at the time – passed off peacefully, with barely a shot fired in anger.

The major political issue dividing Goans in the early 1960s was whether or not to merge with neighbouring

Maharashtra. In the event, 54 percent of the electorate voted to remain a separate Union Territory, though the referendum result probably owed more to the widespread fear that the merger would mean the loss of valuable government jobs (not to mention a stiffening of liquor laws) than any loss of identity.

Full Statehood

However, notions of what it means to be Goan have come very much to the fore since. After being dismissed for years by many in Delhi as a mere dialect, Konkani, the mother tongue of most Goans, was granted Official Language Status in 1987, paving the way for full statehood. Boosted by foreign currency receipts from iron-ore exports and tourism, the economy started to boom in the 1970s and 1980s, and Goans today enjoy one of the country's highest per capita incomes.

In-migration by workers from other Indian regions is rapidly transforming the cultural complexion of Goa. No longer the distant enclave it was at Liberation, the state is now reachable in an easy overnight train ride from Mumbai on the Konkan Railway, inaugurated in 1997, and by flights from most major Indian cities.

The ubiquitous auto-rickshaw

But political life in Panjim over the past decade or so has been blighted by instability and wholesale corruption, with frequent changes of chief ministers and ruling coalitions. The embarrassing imposition of President's Rule by New Delhi in 2004 should have shaken up the state's ruling representatives, but there have been few signs of improvement.

Historical Landmarks

AD973 Goa's first capital, Chandrapura, founded by the Kadambas.

1310 The Sultan of Delhi, Ala-uddin-Khilji, sends his general Malik Kafur on a series of devastating raids into southwest India. The Kadambas' port city, Govapuri, is reduced to ruins.

1367–78 Goa incorporated into the Hindu Vijayangar empire, ushering in a century of peace and prosperity based on the trade of Arab horses and spices.

1472 The Deccani-Muslim Bahmani Sultanate and their successors the Sultans of Bijapur take Goa.

24 November 1510 Afonso de Albuquerque establishes Portuguese rule in the former Bijapuri port capital, Ela, which he renames Goa. The city becomes the capital of a vast maritime trade empire extending from Japan to Europe.

1542 Francis Xavier and the Jesuits arrive in Goa, followed soon after by the Holy Office, or Inquisition.

1570 Lightly defended by only a few hundred Portuguese and their black slaves, Goa holds out against a year-long siege by a massive Bijapuri army.

1580 The Union of Spain and Portugal signals the start of a trade war with the Protestant Dutch and British, who gradually dismantle Portuguese commerce in Asia.

1600s Goa in decline: riven by disease, with its port silted up and trade monopolies taken by rival powers, the city falls into ruins.

1780s After losing chunks of the colony to the Marathas, the Portuguese annex land to the north and south of its core territory: the *Novas Conquistas*.

1827–35 Panjim becomes the new capital of Goa.

1961 'Operation Vijay', the invasion of Goa by Indian forces, brings 451 years of Portuguese rule to an abrupt end.

1987 Goa becomes the 25th State of the Indian Republic.

2004 President's Rule imposed on the State Legislature, focusing national attention on the parlous condition of Goa's ruling body.

WHERE TO GO

Goa's compact size and shape mean even its extremities lie within reach of easy trips by car or motorbike from the resorts. A half-day's drive can take you from a landscape of surf and dunes, through lush rice paddy fields and palm groves to the jungle-covered hills of the interior. Along the way, crowded market towns give way to picturesque Goan villages clustered around whitewashed churches and multi-coloured Hindu temples. Ruined forts and nature reserves are also hidden in the state's hinterland – a world away from the crowds and commercialism of the resorts.

With a little time and a sense of adventure, longer forays outside the state can take you to Gokarna and Hampi, two of southern India's most magical destinations.

CENTRAL GOA

The core of the former Portuguese colony was the so-called *Ilhas*, a cluster of swampy islands and mangrove-lined rivers a short boat ride from the mouth of the Mandovi. These are now far less densely populated than they were in times past, the old capital having been deserted in favour of a healthier site nearer the sea. Along with the spectacular ecclesiastical remains of Old Goa, Panjim (or *Panaji*), the modern capital, is central Goa's main sight, its 19th-century buildings still redolent of the days when the town was a colonial outpost.

Further inland, the forests around the town of Ponda harbour a dozen or more Hindu temples to which Goa's deities were smuggled to escape the Inquisition, as well as several spice plantations and a couple of wildlife sanctuaries covering the mountainous eastern border with Karnataka.

Beach hut at Palolem in the far south

Panjim (Panaji)

Goa's state capital, **Panjim** (also known by its Marathi name, *Panaji*) is spread around the side of a low wooded hill overlooking the mouth of the Mandovi, 10km (6 miles) downriver from the ruins of the former Portuguese city, Old Goa. With a population of only 65,000, it's a middle-sized town by Indian standards – low-rise, relatively uncongested and open on one side to the estuary breezes. Day-tripping foreigners from the north coast resorts come here to shop and eat, and to wander around the backstreets of the atmospheric colonial quarter, while domestic tourists come in even greater numbers for the evening river cruises. But Panjim has made few concessions to tourism and retains its distinctively Goan character, in places with great style.

The town was established at the end of the 18th century, after repeated epidemics forced Old Goa's diminished Portuguese population to decamp to this better-drained, better-aired site. Prior to that, the only buildings of note here were the waterfront palace of the Bijapuri ruler, Yusuf Adil Shah, a late-16th century Dominican college and a string of small hilltop bastions whose cannons crossed fire with those of Reis Magos on the far banks. Dom Manuel Port'e Castro (1826–35) was the governor responsible for reclaiming the marshes on the town's fringes and erecting the grid of civic buildings, squares and broad streets that still unfolds from the waterfront.

After a brief 19th-century boom, fuelled by a temporary surge in the trade of Rajasthani opium, Panjim eased gently into a torpor from which, despite an injection of funds following its promotion to state capital in 1987, it has never fully recovered. Tower blocks have started to spring up on the outskirts, and the Esplanade gained a major facelift ahead of the first International Film Festival of India hosted here in 2004, but the centre still has a relaxed feel, with plenty of period

Panjim Esplanade

character in those enclaves that have escaped the cement mixers. With their peeling colour-washed houses and red-tiled roofs, the districts of Sao Tomé and Fontainhas, in particular, recall the genteel twilight of *India Portuguesa*.

The Esplanade

With its typically Portuguese, double-storeyed façade and high-pitched roofs, the **Secretariat** building midway along Avenida Dom Joao Castro, marooned on a traffic island on the northern edge of town next to the river, is Panjim's oldest surviving building. In its original form the structure served as a waterfront palace for the ruling Sultan of Bijapur, Yusuf Adil Shah, who erected it in 1500 – only 10 years before Goa was invaded by Afonso de Albuquerque. Thereafter, it was converted for use by Portuguese VIPs. The steps that formerly ran to the water's edge would have been the first feel of terra firma for new viceroys arriving

Secretariat façade detail

from Lisbon, and the last for their predecessors embarking on the voyage home. From here, the dignitaries would be escorted upriver to the capital amid much pomp in a flotilla of ceremonial barges.

On the other side of the building, the main entrance preserves its ornamental 16th-century pillars and scrollwork, though the old viceregal coat of arms has been replaced by a white Ashokean wheel – symbol of the Indian Republic. Until recently, Goa's parliament, the Legislative Assembly, sat in session here. However, its notoriously hot-headed members now convene in a much more imposing modern complex on the far bank of the Mandovi River.

The western end of the Esplanade, past the jetty where the old Bombay steamer used to tie up, is dominated by a row of grand Portuguese-era municipal buildings – erected at the height of the opium boom of the 1860s and 1870s. The most impressive of them is the **Menezes Braganza Institute**, established in 1871 and now the site of Panjim's central library (open Mon–Fri 9.30am–1pm, 2–5.30pm). Lining its entrance lobby are panels of striking painted tiles, or *azulejos*, depicting scenes from the patriotic epic of Portugal's best loved poet, Luís Camões, who visited the colony at its height.

Vast sums of public money were spent in the run-up to the prestigious International Film Festival of India (IFFI) in 2004 to transform the **promenade** leading west from the Menezes Braganza Institute. After dark, the walkway is illuminated by rows of ornamental Belgian lights. Contrary to the hopes of the town's grandees, the Cannes seafront it certainly isn't, but the pavement provides a pleasant place for a stroll, especially at sunset.

Church Square

Church Square (also known as the 'Municipal Gardens') forms Panjim's bustling focal point, a short walk back from the riverfront. Its centrepiece is a statue of three Ashokean lions mounted on a 12-m (40-ft) tall pillar, symbolising

The Grandfather of Goan Trance

One of Goa's more illustrious émigrés is commemorated by a rather disturbing statue on a roundabout next to the Secretariat, showing a man waving his outstretched arms over the rigid, supine body of a woman. José Custodio de Faria (1756–1819), a Goan priest who served as confessor to the Portuguese royal family, is credited as the founding father of modern hypnotism – a skill he developed while a political exile in Paris in the 1800s. Dressed in flowing black robes, Faria became a cult figure in the French capital, where he attracted a largely female following. However, his reputation was ruined by rumours he took advantage of his prettier patients during demonstrations. Only after the posthumous publication of his now famous treatise on hypnotism, *On the Causes of Lucid Sleep*, was it ultimately restored. Faria's revolutionary assertion, which contradicted the theories of his more famous contemporary, Franz Anton Mesmer, was that trance was dependent on the will of the patient rather than the result of magnetic forces, thus paving the way for modern notions of the unconscious mind.

Immaculate Conception

'Strength, Unity and Diversity'. A bust of the Portuguese explorer Vasco da Gama used to crown the column, but it was removed after Liberation in 1961 and now resides in the museum at Old Goa.

Sailing serenely above the square, the splendid baroque façade of the **Church of Our Lady of the Immaculate Conception** rises from the head of a flight of crisscrossing steps. Dating from 1541, it's among Goa's oldest surviving colonial buildings, though much of the structure was renewed three centuries later. Sailors used to call here to give thanks for their safe voyage before proceeding to Old Goa, where the giant bell that now tolls mournfully in the church's belfry originated. True to the old colonial decree that all religious buildings (and only religious buildings) should be whitewashed once each year after the monsoons, the church gleams against its backdrop of blue sky, framed by rows of spindly palm trees.

Fontainhas and Sao Tomé

Few corners of Goa evoke the feel of Portuguese times as vividly as the enclave southeast of Panjim church, running along the left bank of Ourem Creek. This eastern flank of the town, stacked up the sides of leafy Altinho Hill, was its main residential area in the 19th century. However, since then the districts of **Fontainhas** and **Sao Tomé** have fallen on hard times. Goa's inheritance laws have forced many of the old properties in them to be divided between different family members, many of whom have emigrated, leaving their former homes to the mercy of poorer relatives and the monsoon rains. Yet the aura of dilapidation only serves to heighten the sense of an area locked in a Lusitanian time warp.

More than 40 years after Liberation, Portuguese is still the first language of most of its older residents. Walking around the back lanes, past the colour-washed houses with their doorways and window surrounds picked out with whitewash, you'll see shopfronts carrying names like De Souza, Pinto and Fernandes, and elderly *senhoras* chatting from verandas filled with bougainvillea and the chirping of caged finches.

The Portuguese ambience is most marked in the pretty little *praça* fronting the **Chapel of St Sebastian** in Fontainhas. Each November, this is where the district's families gather to celebrate the feast day, or *festa*, of St John, when *rissois de peixe* (fish cutlets), the latest family gossip from Lisbon and Konani *dulpods* are the order of the day. The chapel itself houses a particularly eerie crucifix, whose penetrating gaze used to bear down on those terrified souls hauled before the Inquisitors of Old Goa. On a lighter note, local artisans have revived the Portuguese tradition of painted tiles, or *azulejos*; you can watch them at work in a tiny studio just off the square.

Colourful Sao Tomé

Museums

Panjim's other noteworthy memento of the Inquisition is housed in Goa's little-visited **State Archaeological Museum** (open Mon–Fri 9.30am–1pm, 2–5.30pm; admission fee), languishing amid a patch of wasteland on the opposite side of Ourem Creek from Fontainhas. On the first floor, an ornately carved Italian-style table and its set of matching chairs were once used by the Inquisitors who sat in judgement of suspected heretics. Aside from some fine Jain bronzes reclaimed from smugglers by local customs men, there's little else of more than passing interest here, the bulk of Goa's historic artefacts having been gathered in a museum at Old Goa.

Hidden away in a village near the fast-expanding suburb of **Porvorim**, across the Mandovi River from Panjim, the

---

Carnival

Just before the start of Lent Panjim plays host to Goa's jubilant Carnival, a three-day round of processions, costumed dances, street music and general mayhem. Though considerably more restrained than comparable events in the Caribbean and South America, the occasion is largely good-natured and a lot of fun to watch. That said, onlookers should be prepared to be pelted with perfumed powder bombs and exploding '*cocotes*' of flour and water.

Starting on *Sabato Gordo* ('Fat Saturday'), Carnival's showpiece is a grand parade of floats led by 'King Momo', who declares the event open and instructs the assembled onlookers to make merry. However, the past decade or so has seen the festivities grow increasingly commercialised, with corporate sponsors hijacking the float parade. This has provoked heated condemnation from some quarters, not least the Goan Church, which in 1993 banned Roman Catholic girls from participating. Hindi movies have also done the Goan Carnival a disservice by misrepresenting it as something of a sexual free-for-all.

Houses of Goa Museum (open Tues–Sun 10am–7.30pm; admission fee) is a privately owned exhibition showcasing the architectural richness of Goa's stately homes. It occupies an eccentric triangular-shaped building which was designed by the museum's co-founder, internationally acclaimed architect Gerard De Cunha. The themed displays inside, divided over four floors interconnected by winding staircases, begin with a pictorial outline of Goan history, then move on to cover the style trends and extravagant décor of traditional Goan *palacios*, from ornamental gateposts to rooftop finials, oystershell windows and carved furniture.

Houses of Goa Museum

Dona Paula

Dona Paula is a tiny resort tucked away on the south side of the headland dividing the mouths of the Mandovi and Zuari rivers. Only 9km (5 miles) from Panjim, it's basically a suburb of the capital, popular mainly with bus parties of Indian day trippers. However, as a beach destination, the village has little to recommend it, with no clean sand or open space to speak of. Most foreign visitors who end up here do so on cut-price charters, based in one or other of a string of small hotels hastily erected in the boom of the early 1990s.

The one reason you might wish to venture out to Dona Paula is to catch the ferry across the Zuari to Mormugao port (four times daily) – a rollicking ride through choppy surf.

Inside the church of St Cajetan

▶ Old Goa

At the height of its splendour in the late 16th and 17th centuries, the former Portuguese capital of Goa, 10km (6 miles) upriver from modern Panjim, was a city of extraordinary magnificence. Contemporary engravings and chronicles delineate a skyline bristling with baroque cathedrals and church spires, vast paved piazzas and a port heaving with the spoils of empire: spices from southeast Asia, thoroughbred horses from Arabia, Malabari pearls, Ceylonese precious stones, gold from the East African ports and coinage from all across the known world. Bigger even than Lisbon and London in its day, it was the first great colonial metropolis – the nucleus of a trade network spanning all the way from the Pacific rim to the eastern Atlantic.

Yet life in the colony was notoriously fragile and short. Disease and death were ever present and could strike at any moment, engendering a culture of hedonism and excess that far surpassed the most liberal cultures of Europe. Travellers regularly talked of the drunkenness and debauchery indulged in by all levels of society, from the *mestiço* soldiery to the opulently dressed aristocratic women who drugged their husbands while engaging in illicit affairs.

Goa eventually declined as dramatically, and suddenly, as it sprang from the Konkani laterite. A combination of epidemics, a silted-up harbour and the rise of Portugal's rival powers elsewhere in the Orient strangled its trade and depleted the population beyond recovery. Today, it's almost impossible to imagine the city as it once looked. Jungle has reclaimed its streets, leaving only the domes and towers of the capital's vast churches to soar above the forest like visions of a Lost World.

Even so, **Old Goa** (as the site is called nowadays) fully deserves its status as the state's prime visitor attraction. As well as the surviving cathedral, churches and convents, the tomb of St Francis Xavier *(see page 21)* in the majestic Basilica of Bom Jesus attracts Christians from all over India, while a pair of well-stocked museums showcase historic artefacts from both the Portuguese and pre-colonial periods.

Old Goa's most impressive monuments are ranged around an enormous expanse of grass where the city's main square, the **Terreiro de Gales**, once lay. During the feast of St Francis Xavier at the beginning of December, its lawns accommodate tens of thousands of pilgrims who sleep here waiting for Mass at dawn on the first day of the festival. However, in Portuguese times military

You can comfortably cover Old Goa's highlights in three or four hours. But don't underestimate the heat, which is far more humid and oppressive than on the beach. Bring plenty of drinking water, a hat and respectable clothes for visiting the churches.

parades, public hangings and burnings of heretics by the Inquisition were what attracted the crowds.

To gain a sense of how Old Goa's architecture evolved over the centuries, start your tour at the northeast edge of the site, under the **Viceroy's Arch**. This triumphal gateway, the last surviving remnant of Goa's medieval ramparts, spanned the city's main artery, the **Rua Direita**, which ran in a straight line from the harbourside through the square. It was erected in 1599 by Francisco Da Gama as a memorial to his grandfather, the explorer Vasco Da Gama, who discovered the sea route around the Cape of Good Hope and across the Indian Ocean. His coat of arms adorns the side of the arch facing the river; on the opposite flank, a figure holding the Bible stands with his foot on a recumbent native, symbolising the victory of Christianity over heathen ignorance.

Viceroy's Arch

Only one small fragment is left of Yusuf Adil Shah's former Muslim city: a grey basalt door jamb, decorated with Hindu motifs (suggesting the original masonry was probably pillaged from an even earlier Hindu temple). It stands on a plinth down a side road off the Rua Direita, next to the **Convent of St Cajetan**, where the Santo Officio, or Goan Inquisition, once had its headquarters. A vivid account of the horrors inflicted on the unfortunate souls imprisoned in its dungeons has survived in the memoirs of a French physician, Charles Dellon, incarcerated here on trumped-up charges of blasphemy in 1673.

Dellon recounted the macabre theatricality with which the mass autos-da-fé (literally 'trials of faith') were conducted, and the various tortures used to extract confessions of heresy and witchcraft.

In all, over 16,000 people were arrested by the Inquisition between 1560 and 1774, for crimes ranging from 'eating rice without salt' to 'refusing to eat pork', and

For a wonderful panoramic view over Old Goa, scale the steps leading up to the Church of Our Lady of the Mount, on a hilltop east of St Cajetan (below).

'selling arms to infidels'. Although most of them were Hindus, 71 percent of those eventually executed were new converts of Jewish descent who had fled to Goa to escape the reach of the Inquisition in Iberia.

Adjacent to the convent, the luxuriously domed **Church of St Cajetan** is said to have been modelled on St Peter's in Rome. It was built between 1612 and 1661 by the Theatine Order of missionary priests, who settled in Goa after being refused entry to their original destination, the Sultanate of Galconda. St Cajetan is renowned for its ornate woodwork, notably the pulpit and sumptuously carved panels around the main altar inside.

Sé Cathedral and Church of St Francis of Assisi

Dominating the north side of the square, the **Sé Cathedral** is the largest church in Asia and an emphatic symbol of Portuguese power at the empire's 17th-century zenith. Although most of the building conforms to textbook Jesuit style, its twin, square campaniles are a definably Goan addition. One of them collapsed after being struck by lightning in 1776; the other houses the huge Golden Bell, or *Sino do Ouro*, whose tolling used to announce the terrible autos-da-fé held by the Inquisition in front of it. Inside, a wonderful reredos (screen) covered in gold leaf depicts scenes from the martyrdom of St Catherine, patron saint of the city. Worshippers also pray at a small chapel on the north wall housing the *Cruz dos Milagros*, or Miraculous Cross, on which an apparition of Christ is believed to have appeared in 1619.

Sé Cathedral: façade detail

Next door to the Sé, the **Church of St Francis of Assisi** dates from 1661, but incorporates fragments of an earlier building. These include a wonderful Manueline doorway featuring the kind of nautical motifs popular during the Portuguese discoveries: twisting ropes, globes and the Greek cross (which used to adorn the sails of Portuguese explorers' *caravelas*). Handsomely carved tombstones of the nobility line the flagstones of the sumptuously restored interior, which features some especially fine murals of Islamic-influenced floral patterns.

Archaeological Museum and Chapel of St Catherine

Old Goa's **Archaeological Museum** (open daily 10am–4pm), which abuts the Church of St Francis of Assisi, occupies part of a former Franciscan monastery. In addition to many fine pieces of temple sculpture that were salvaged from the city's ruins, its prime exhibits are the 60 portraits of Portuguese viceroys lined up in the first-floor gallery. These graphically demonstrate the change in dress styles over the years from the robust military garb of the early 16th century to the effeminate ruffs and lace of later generations – an evolution which mirrors Old Goa's own descent into decadence.

The very first church to be built in the colony, commissioned by Afonso de Albuquerque himself as an act of thanksgiving after the defeat of Bijapur's Muslim army on St Catherine's Day, 1510, stands a short way from the museum. A papal bull granted the modest mud-and-straw structure that preceded this one with cathedral status in 1534, though it was subsequently repealed when the Sé was completed. The **Chapel of St Catherine**'s twin towers prefigure those of its bigger sister across the square, and are the first known examples of what over time came to create a distinctively Goan style of church architecture.

The Basilica of Bom Jesus

Old Goa's majestic **Basilica of Bom Jesus** is famous as the site of St Francis Xavier's mausoleum, but it's a beautiful building in its own right, blending neo-classical restraint with baroque exuberance to great effect. Designed to inspire awe among the new converts of the *Estado da India*, the proportions and decorative detail of the façade typify the flamboyance of the late Renaissance.

The interior is equally impressive, centred on an enormous gold reredos dedicated to St Ignatius Loyola, founder of the Jesuit Order. The Jesuits were the first to undertake large-scale missionary activity in Portugal's new Asian possessions, and

Basilica of Bom Jesus

their most successful emissary was the Basque priest, Francis Xavier *(see page 21)*. Housed in a small chapel in the basilica's south transept, his supposedly incorruptible remains are Old Goa's most revered relic. They're enshrined in a Florentine-style tomb endowed by the Medicis in the 1690s, made from precious marbles and jaspers brought from Italy. Bronze panels illustrating scenes from the saint's life adorn the base. The glass-sided casket itself is made of solid silver and was once studded with jewels.

Every 10 years on the feast day of St Francis Xavier, the body, which for centuries showed no signs of decay, is lowered to ground level and becomes the focus of a mass pilgrimage drawing pilgrims from all over the Christian world. Since it started to show signs of decomposition (in truth it's a grizzly sight these days), some in the Church have suggested the 'Exposition' should be stopped – but the mass popularity of the last one in 2004 seems to have silenced the event's critics for the time being.

Holy Hill

Some of the former city's oldest monuments are dotted along the lane running west from the basilica, in the area known as **Holy Hill**. Founded in 1601, the **Convent of Santa Monica** was once the only nunnery in Goa, and it remains in use today. Ring the bell and one of the sisters will show you around the gloomy church, with its Miraculous Cross. Next door, the **Museum of Christian Art** (open daily 9.30am–5pm; admission fee) displays a collection of processional crosses, clerical robes and carved wooden icons dating from the 17th and 18th centuries.

Other than a crumbling belltower (one of Old Goa's more spectral sights), little remains of the old **Augustinian Monastery** opposite Santa Monica. But not far from the convent, the **Chapel of Our Lady of the Rosary** is remarkably well preserved considering it was already in use when Francis Xavier first came in 1542. The church, erected on the spot from which Afonso de Albuquerque directed the battle with the Bijapuri forces, is the finest complete example of Manueline architecture in Old Goa; note the rope mouldings around the windows and doorway. Inside is the finely carved marble tombstone of Catarina a Piro, allegedly the first European woman to have set foot in the colony; she eloped here with the man who would later become governor, though they were only married on her deathbed.

Across the Mandovi to Divar Island

Chorao and Divar Islands

From the jetty below Old Goa's Viceroy's Arch, a river ferry chugs across the Mandovi to **Divar Island**. Surrounded by rice fields, its only village, **Piedade**, comprises 100 or so quaint Portuguese-era houses wrapped around the foot of a wooded hill, on top of which the Church of Our Lady of Compassion affords a superb panorama over Old Goa and its surrounding countryside.

A second ferry joins Divar to neighbouring **Chorao Island**, whose southwestern point has been designated as the **Salim Ali Bird Sanctuary**. As well as being one of Goa's ornithological hotspots, the mangrove swamps and mudflats fringing the river banks here are prowled by mugger crocodiles, thought to have first been introduced by the Bijapuri sultan Yusuf Adil Shah to prevent his slaves swimming to freedom. Excursion boats transport tourists to the sanctuary and beyond to the Cambarjua Canal, where the greatest concentration of crocodiles is to be found. Seats on the boats may be booked through agents in north Goa's bigger resorts.

Ponda and Its Temples

The town of **Ponda**, in the dead centre of Goa on the main Panjim–Bangalore highway, serves as a hub for the region's iron-ore industry. It's also renowned as the home of the state's favourite tipple, Kingfisher beer, though traffic fumes and congestion are likely to leave a more lasting impression than the aroma of toasted hops. The only sight to speak of is the compact **Jama Masjid** mosque, 2km (1½ miles) west on the outskirts. Erected by the Bijapuri sultan Ibrahim Adil Shah in 1560, the building and its adjacent ablutions tank are among the last surviving vestiges of Muslim Goa, the rest having been dismantled by the Portuguese after the rout of 1510.

The zeal with which the colonisers persecuted native religions and beliefs in the 16th and 17th centuries forced the custodians of Goa's ancient Hindu temples to flee inland, across the Zuari River beyond the margins of Portuguese territory. A dozen or more of these shrines still stand in the hidden valleys around Ponda. They're grouped into two main clusters: one 8–10km (5–6 miles) north of the town and the other 5km (3 miles) west. If you're pushed for time, stick to the grandest of the bunch, the **Sri Manguesh Temple**, 9km (5½ miles) north on the highway near the village of Priol. Dedicated to a beneficent form of the god Shiva, the building is a quintessentially Goan, hybrid hotchpotch of Moghul

Rama and Sita at Sri Manguesh

domes and baroque flourishes, culminating in an octagonal sanctuary tower. If you're lucky, the priest will allow you a glimpse of the solid gold deity inside, framed by an ornate silver door.

A couple of kilometres (1½ miles) south, near Nardol village, the **Sri Mahalsa Temple** is this area's other important shrine. It houses the consort of the god Vishnu, Lakshmi, goddess of wealth and prosperity, in her black-faced form, Mahalsa. Like Sri Manguesh, this temple, visited in large numbers by pilgrims from outside the state, is very wealthy and embellished accordingly, with some fine woodcarvings and sculptures depicting Vishnu in his 10 incarnations. It also holds an impressive lamp tower, or *deepmal*, on which hundreds of tiny oil lamps are illuminated during festivals – a magical sight.

Spice Plantations

Spices have been farmed commercially in Goa for hundreds of years, alongside other important cash crops such as cashews, breadfruit, bananas, mangoes and areca nuts (consumed in vast quantities in India as *paan masala*). If you've only ever encountered such exotic produce in their dried forms or on supermarket shelves, then a visit to one of the spice plantations tucked away in the forest outside Ponda will come as a revelation.

Highlights of these guided tours, which can be arranged through operators in any of the resorts, include watching the areca harvesters swinging monkey-style from tree to tree, and the slap-up Goan meal served on a banana leaf at the end (invariably with a peg of local *feni*).

The **Sahakari Farm**, only 1km (½ mile) east of Ponda on NH-4, is easy to find on your own if you'd prefer not to go as part of an organised tour. In addition to all the usual spices, the Sahakari family cultivate vanilla, tea and coffee using organic farming methods.

Wildlife Sanctuaries

Heading inland from Ponda, it isn't long before the shadowy profile of the Western Ghats starts to dominate the horizon. The mountains, part of a range that runs the whole length of India's western edge, tracks the border with neighbouring Karnataka state, forming a natural boundary between the well-watered coastal strip and the drier, volcanic uplands of the Deccan Plateau.

At an average elevation of 800m (2,625ft), they're large enough to obstruct the eastward flow of the monsoon weather systems, and receive a colossal amount of rainfall as a result. Ever-

Areca plucker on a Ponda spice plantation

green and moist deciduous forest cloaks the sides of the mountains, supporting wildlife ranging from Indian bison (*gaur*), to jungle civets, elephant, antelope, monkeys and dozens of species of snakes – though no longer tigers. Sadly, pressure from grazing, settlements, loggers and the iron-ore industry has cut huge swathes through this exquisite forest, though a couple of tracts survive and are now protected as wildlife sanctuaries.

Covering only 8 sq km (3 sq miles), **Bondla**, 52km (32 miles) east of Panjim, is the smallest of them. The park sees more than its share of visitors thanks to the rather scruffy zoo at its centre (open Fri–Wed 9.30am–5.30pm; admission fee), where bus parties gawp at some sad-looking animals captured from the surrounding jungle.

A far more enticing prospect for serious wildlife enthusiasts is the much larger **Bhagwan Mahaveer Sanctuary**, further east on the main highway, which encompasses 240 sq km (93 sq miles) of jungle-covered hills, valleys and canyons. The main gateway is an Interpretative Centre at **Molem** (open daily 9.30am–5.30pm), which provides a lacklustre rundown of local flora and fauna.

However, for a real taste of the area's splendours you'll have to venture off the main road and into the forest proper. Lying close to the sanctuary's borders, two attractions – one man-made, the other natural – provide plenty of incentive to do so.

Tambdi Surla

Precious few remnants of pre-colonial Goa survived the iconoclastic excesses of the Portuguese era, but at **Tambdi Surla**, 12km (7 miles) north of Molem, a lone Hindu shrine somehow managed to escape the attention of the zealots of the Inquisition. Erected by the Kadamba dynasty, who ruled Goa between the 10th and 14th centuries, the **Mahadeva Temple** rises from a clearing deep in the forest, enfolded by ridges of wooded hills.

Tambdi Surla

Precisely why this remote site was chosen by the Hindu kings remains a mystery, but the shrine, made from weather-resistant basalt imported from across the Western Ghats, was obviously of some importance. It is dedicated to Shiva, in the form of a phallic *lingam*, and richly carved with geometric patterns and deities. The finest stonework – an intricate lotus motif – lines the ceiling of the main sanctuary hall.

Dudhsagar

The waterfalls at **Dudhsagar**, near Goa's eastern border in the wildest part of the Bhagwan Mahaveer Sanctuary, are the second-highest in India. Measuring 600m (656ft) from head to foot, they're a spectacular sight at any time of year, but especially just after the monsoon rains in October and November, when water levels are at their highest.

Dudhsagar Falls

Getting to them can be something of an adventure. Although the main Goa–Hyderabad train line slices straight over the falls, there are no day-return services and no sealed roads to Dudhsagar, so instead you have to drive there in a Jeep via a rutted forest track – a memorable ride through some luxuriant teak forest. Emerging from the world of buttressed roots, creepers and giant trunks, you'll be rewarded with a spectacular view over the Ghats and down to the plains. Rock pools at the foot of the falls provide safe bathing provided the river isn't in spate.

Trips to Dudhsagar are offered as packages from the resorts. Alternatively, make your own transport arrangements, hiring a taxi to Molem, where Jeep drivers wait for custom outside the railway station.

Baga beach

NORTH GOA

North Goa is divided between the predominantly Christian *taluka* of Bardez, part of the first territory grabbed by the Portuguese in the 16th century, and Hindu-majority Pernem district, which was conquered in the second wave of colonial expansion in the 1700s. Separating the two, the Chapora River also forms a fault line for tourism: whereas the Bardez coast is lined with package resorts, the shoreline of Pernem has remained largely unscarred by the cement mixers. This may be about to change with the completion of a major road bridge across the Chapora (formerly you had to traverse the river in a slow ferry), but for the time being it's still the case that the further north you travel, the quieter the beaches get.

Mapusa, a bustling little town roughly 15–20 minutes' drive inland from the resorts, is this area's main hub. Try to time your visit for Friday mornings, when a colourful fresh-produce market springs up in the centre.

Mapusa

Mapusa – pronounced '*map*-sa' – is the district headquarters of Bardez *taluka*. As the principal source of supplies for north Goa's scattered villages, the town stands in marked contrast to the razzmatazz of the beach resorts, only a short taxi ride west. Heaped up the sides of a low hill, its largely modern centre is unrelentingly hot and drab, and holds little of interest for visitors. However, you should make time for the colourful **market** that erupts on Fridays in the grid of ◄ streets east of the main square. Dressed in vibrant saris, women from the surrounding hamlets set up stalls of garden produce under ragged parasols, haggling with local housewives between exchanges of gossip. Huge plantains are a local speciality, grown in plantations at nearby Moira. As at the Anjuna flea market, you'll also come across Lamani traders, wrapped from head to toe in hand-woven rainbow textiles, mirror-work and jewellery.

An essential stop in the heart of the market is F.R. Xavier's, where the middle classes recover from their shopping over patties, samosas and tea. Bibliophiles should also seek out the Other India Bookshop, one of Goa's best-stocked bookstores, tucked away north of the market area behind Mapusa Clinic.

Stallholder at Mapusa market

Fort Aguada

As the gateway to the former capital at Old Goa, the mouth of the Mandovi was of vital strategic importance in colonial times. Eager to ensure no other attacking force should have as easy an approach through it as Afonso de Albuquerque's fleet did in 1510, the Portuguese fortified both headlands overlooking the river mouth in the mid-16th century, together with similar points all along the Goan coast. Designed to give any enemy ships that ventured too close a solid pounding with 200 cannons, the most impressive in this chain of defences was **Fort Aguada**, which still stands on the promontory dividing the Mandovi from Calangute beach. A sprawling complex of dry moats, sloping walls and turreted battlements, the square-shaped citadel at its heart is centred on a vaulted cistern that provided the first source of fresh drinking water to ships newly arrived from Lisbon, hence the name. The site's other dis-

Reis Magos church

tinctive feature is a pair of lighthouses, the older of which – a squat, conical structure – was erected in 1864. You can climb up to the ramparts near by for a superb panoramic view of the coast.

Reis Magos

Predating Fort Aguada by half a century, a second, smaller fort crowns the headland jutting into the narrowest stretch of the Mandovi, almost opposite Panjim at the village of **Reis Magos**. It too has dramatically sloping walls falling to a steep escarpment at the waterside, where one of Goa's oldest churches still nestles in the shadow of the old ramparts. Built in 1555, the church was named after the Three Magi, or Kings of the Nativity, and originally served a Franciscan seminary, long since disappeared. In common with the Adil Shah's palace on the opposite bank of the Mandovi, dignitaries arriving in or departing from the colony by ship used to spend a night or two here en route to or from the city up river.

Some hint of the site's former prominence is given by the presence on the church's whitewashed gable of Portugal's royal insignia and coat of arms. Inside, tombstones of viceroys and other nobility pave the floor, among them one belonging to Dom Luís de Ataide, the military commander whose vastly outnumbered defensive force held off the Muslim counter-attack of 1570 – a famous victory that cemented Portuguese rule in Goa.

Sinquerim and Candolim

Sinquerim, the southernmost portion of the vast beach sweeping north from the foot of Fort Aguada, is where luxury tourism gained its first toehold in Goa. Still going strong after more than three decades, Taj Group's Fort Aguada Beach Resort was laid out above an unusual historic landmark: a circular cannon emplacement at the end of a long stone jetty. As a prelude to the expanse of white sand shimmering north, it presides over a spot as picturesque as any on the north coast, but one little enhanced by the ranks of shacks, sunloungers and parasols sprawling to the horizon.

The first major agglomeration of holiday complexes springs up at **Candolim**, a couple of kilometres (a mile or so) further north. In the 17th and 18th centuries, the palm-shaded dunes behind the beach here were settled by Goan aristocrats who had grown wealthy in the service of their colonial overlords, but preferred the fishing village's fresher sea air to the less salubrious confines of the capital. Some of their elegant neo-classical *palacios* still hide among the co-conut groves, but they're far outnumbered these days by the hotels, time-share blocks and restaurants along the village's busy main artery, CHOGM Road (Commonwealth Heads of Government Marg), named after the 1983 conference for which it and the Taj resort were originally built.

Less brash and crowded than neighbouring Calangute, yet within easy reach of the airport, Candolim is a popular des-tination for middle-aged European sun-seekers, increasing numbers of whom are snapping up retirement flats in the area. The nightlife is correspondingly sedate, but the bars and restaurants tend to be family run and more welcoming than those further up the main Candolim–Calangute strip.

Calangute

Step off a transit bus in **Calangute** and your first impression of Goa will be none too promising. Although much less built up than resorts of comparable importance on the Span-ish or Turkish coasts, the 'village' and its environs have been overwhelmed with development on a scale unseen elsewhere in the state. In full swing, the main market area in particular can get horrendously chaotic and polluted, while the beachfront itself, a prime target for bus parties of visi-tors from other Indian states, is deluged with day trippers, hawkers and litter.

It's all a far cry from more genteel times, when Calangute served as a hot-season retreat for Mapusa and Panjim's middle classes. They would come here in the blazing heat of May for the breeze and fresh seafood at Souza Lobo seafront restau-rant. This was also where the first dope-smoking, skinny-dipping hippy tourists to Goa congregated in the 1960s and 1970s, living in palm-thatched huts on the sand where they were something of a tourist attraction themselves.

Dusk at Calangute beach

Despite the mess and commercialism of the modern resort, a few pockets of what Calangute used to be survive on its fringes. Head south for 10 minutes from the main beachfront and you'll come to the traditional fishing quarter, where rows of wooden outriggers lurk in the dunes. Most of the diminishing stocks that their owners haul from the surf ends up in the local **covered market**, at the end of Calangute's main street opposite the Hindu temple, sold by fisherwomen in old-fashioned saris tied *dhoti*-style around their legs. On Saturday mornings, the whole market, together with traders from across Bardez, reconvenes in a shady outdoor plot near the post office.

Baga
Baga village occupies the far northern end of Calangute beach, an area these days given over almost entirely to European charter tourism. In peak season, its fabled golden

sands, ending at a spit where painted boats line up along the banks of a tidal creek, are barely visible beneath a carpet of roasting foreign bodies, serviced by armies of Karnatakan hawkers, fruit-sellers and itinerant masseurs. By night, the lane running parallel with the beach is transformed into a gaudily lit strip to which a fleet of Maruti taxis ferries tourists from the resort complexes on Baga's outskirts.

At the epicentre of this East-meets-West mayhem is Tito's, Goa's most famous nightclub *(see page 87)*, nowadays hemmed in by karaoke bars and sophisticated restaurants where, on weekend nights, package tourists from northern Europe mingle with well-heeled fun-seekers from Bangalore and Mumbai.

Anjuna

Once over the ugly concrete box bridge spanning Baga creek, the lane skirting the river plunges into the palm forest to reach **Anjuna**, the next village up the coast. When charter tourism

Ingo's Night Market

One of the highlights of north Goa's tourist scene is the market held each Saturday evening at Arpora, 3km (2 miles) inland from Baga on the main Calangute–Anjuna road. The brainchild of a German expatriate called Ingo, it hosts the same gamut of traders who show up every week at the Anjuna flea market, along with a stronger showing of foreign stallholders selling funky party gear and other designer souvenirs. Live bands perform on a stage, and there's a row of counters dishing up fresh food and drink. The event kicks off just after sunset and ends at around 11pm.

Note that a rival night market called Macy's operates on land closer to Baga, but it's not a patch on Ingo's – though your taxi driver (who will get a commission for taking you there) may insist otherwise.

started to squeeze the hippy contingent out of Calangute, it was to here the party scene shifted. The big full-moon raves that made it famous in the 1980s and 1990s are a rarity these days, but Anjuna remains the spiritual home of 'Goan trance' music, pulling in a steady line of long-staying, hard-partying foreigners each winter (the majority young Israelis fresh out of national service in the Occupied Territories).

Anjuna's other claim to fame is its **flea market**. On Wednesdays, traders and tourists from all over the state flock to a coconut grove at the southern end of the beach for what must be one of Asia's most colourful and quirky jamborees. It started life as a proper flea market, where north Goa's hippy population would meet up to trade books, clothes, food, drugs and travelling tales.

Contrary to appearances, swimming isn't all that safe from the middle of Anjuna beach, as it suffers from a dangerous undertow at certain phases of the tide. You're better off in the more sheltered cove at its far southern end.

Since then, like most things in Goa, the event has grown beyond recognition and become much more commercialised, but as a spectacle it remains without parallel in India, mixing package holidaymakers from northern Europe with traders from Tibet to the Tamil south,

Puppet for sale at Anjuna flea market

along with snake charmers, sadhus (Indian holy men), beggars and costumed bulls from the four corners of the subcontinent.

As the flea market starts to peter out at around 5pm, there's a general drift up the beach to the Shore Bar for sunset, and then on to the Club Paradiso, where you can hear Goan trance in its definitive setting, played to a crowd of stoned foreigners on a snazzily decorated open-air dance floor.

Vagator

Thickets of motorcycles and scooters parked on the clifftops north of Anjuna flag pathways to the trio of palm-backed coves where most of this area's foreign visitors hang out. **Ozran Vagator**, the first and largest of them, is the site of an iconic face carved from the rocks near a freshwater spring. Behind it, a row of shacks and coconut terraces are overshadowed by the famous Nine Bar, whose thumping sound system pumps out the latest trance mixes from Amsterdam and Tel Aviv to accompany the sunsets.

Vagator village proper begins a couple of kilometres (a mile or so) further north, scattered around a tangle of leafy lanes. It is a relaxed, pretty place of red-tiled houses with verandas opening onto tree-filled gardens, though the coach park overlooking spectacular **Big Vagator beach**, at the top of the village, gets inundated with noisy picnickers during the season and is best avoided.

Chapora and Siolim

Dominating this gorgeous stretch of coast from atop a parched laterite hill are the ramparts of **Chapora Fort**. The stronghold, visible for miles in all directions, was erected by the Portuguese in 1617, but fell a hundred or so years later to the Maratha chieftain Sambhaji, whose armies allegedly scaled its steep red-brown walls by attaching ropes to sticky-toed monitor lizards. A walled graveyard in front of the fort encloses Muslim tombstones dating from precolonial times, when the site was known as 'Shah Pura' (from which it derives its present name).

From the battlements is a magnificent view up the coast of Pernem to the north, and down over the fishing anchorage and settlement of **Chapora** itself. A druggy tourist scene has grown up in the bazaar of this ramshackle village, where several cafés serve as hang-outs for small-scale Russian

Chapora Fort

mafiosi – explaining the predominance of Cyrillic script. A more sedate and respectable atmosphere prevails at **Siolim**, up the estuary from Chapora. Before the huge river bridge was built, this handsome village of old Portuguese houses, nestling under a lush canopy of palm and mango trees, was where travellers heading north had to catch the ferry. Now, you can complete the journey in a matter of minutes, which looks set to have a dramatic impact on the hitherto little-visited region to the north. The best reason to pause in Siolim is for the elegant *casa palacio*, a 300-year-old Portuguese-era mansion converted into a heritage hotel *(see page 132)*.

The Far North: Pernem

The far northern district of Goa, **Pernem**, wasn't conquered by the Portuguese until 1778, and even today the influence of Christianity remains less marked than that of Hinduism. Along the roadsides, brightly painted temples and saris far outnumber whitewashed churches and tailored European dress. Tourism, too, has made less of an impact along this beautiful stretch of coast. From the sandy spit that curls into the estuary opposite Chapora Fort, you can walk all the way

Hand net fishing in Morjim

to Arambol, a couple of hours north, along an unbroken beach without passing a single concrete eyesore.

There are, however, plenty of shacks and bamboo hut camps dotted along the beach. A steady flow of Maruti vans trundles up from the Calangute–Baga belt each day to the largest of them, at **Morjim** *(Morji)*, the most southerly stretch of

Traffic at Aswem

a beautiful 9-km (6-mile) spread of white sand. Close to the line of shacks at the roadhead, small fenced enclosures mark the sites of Olive Ridley marine turtle nests. Dolphins also put in regular appearances here, and if you're lucky you might catch sight of a white-bellied fish eagle diving for mackerel in the surf.

Passing fragrant cashew groves with glimpses through the coconut trees of white dunes and waves, the coast road winding north from Morjim is among the prettiest in the state. You can pull over at several points for a dip. Shaded by palm trees on raised laterite terraces, a cluster of beach restaurants at **Aswem** *(Ashwem)* offers safe bathing and a fancy French-run café; and at **Mandrem** there's a fully fledged holiday camp, complete with disco floor and groovy bar, made entirely of thatch and bamboo.

Not until **Arambol** *(Harmal)*, the largest coastal settlement in Pernem, do you run into significant numbers of tourists. Spread behind a vast sandy beach, the mixed Christian and Hindu village is popular mainly with an alternative crowd. Accommodation and eating options are basic by the standards of resorts further south, but the beaches are idyllic, especially at sunset. From Arambol's main beachfront area, walk north around the headland to **Paliem** (aka 'lakeside') beach, behind which a freshwater pond is lined with sulphurous mud which the local hippies smother over themselves – much to the evident delight of Indian visitors.

A much less frequented beach lies a 20-minute drive further north of Arambol at **Kerim** *(Querim)*. Backed by rows of wispy casuarina trees, it's not as picturesque as those further south, but remains deserted most of the time. The few visitors who stop here tend to do so in order to kill time while they wait for the ferry across the nearby Terekol River, which can only be crossed at low tide.

The ride takes you to a tiny enclave of Goa on the opposite shore, cowering at the far southwestern tip of Maharashtra, where a lonely Portuguese fort stares southwards down the coast. **Terekol** was originally built by the Marathas in the early 1700s, but was absorbed into the European colony soon after. Other than a couple of ineffectual mutinies against Portuguese rule, it saw little action and nowadays serves as a sensitively restored, *pousada*-style heritage hotel *(see page 130)*. Non-residents are welcome inside to enjoy the rapturous views from the hotel terrace, and for a walk round the red laterite ramparts.

Terekol Fort and view

Putting to sea from Palolem beach

SOUTH GOA

A magnificent sweep of sand stretches south virtually from the foot of the Dabolim Plateau, dominated by the civil airport and adjacent naval aerodrome. Arriving in Goa by plane, it's possible to clear customs and be swimming from this wonderful beach within an hour and a half. Dotted through the dense palm forest behind it is a string of mainly Christian fishing villages, together with a chain of ultra-luxurious resort hotels that between them hold accommodation to suit most pockets. Further south still, beyond the Cabo da Rama peninsula, a much more indented coastline, backed by low hills, shelters a succession of hidden beaches, among them Agonda and Palolem, the jewels in the crown of Goa's coastline.

Margao (Madgaon)

With a burgeoning population of over 100,000, **Margao** (also known as *Madgaon*) is Goa's second-largest town. It can feel frenetic compared with the resorts just a 10-minute scooter ride west, but given a little time yields plenty of distinctive Goan character. Just north of the main square, or Municipal Gardens, a dozen or so blocks of 18th- and 19th-century Portuguese houses are the state's richest single storehouse of vernacular colonial architecture. Its centrepiece is the **Church of the Holy Spirit**, built in 1675 with a textbook late-baroque edifice and a grand whitewashed façade. In the middle of the square outside, the monumental cross facing it has an ornately decorated base showing scenes from the Easter story.

A fine view over Margao's colonial enclave is to be had from Monte Hill, reached via the Calçada de Nossa Senhora de Piedade, which strikes up the slope directly behind the Church of the Holy Spirit.

Coconuts

Along with fishing and rice cultivation, coconuts *(cocos nucifera)* have always formed the backbone of Goa's economy. Around 40 million are consumed in the state every year (that's one per day per family), most often mixed with fish curry. One-sixth of the local population is engaged in tending the trees, which not only form a cornerstone of the Goan diet but also provide coir for making sea-water-resistant rope (an essential component for traditional fishing outriggers), thatch for shade and huts, wood for construction and baby coconuts for sale to the cosmetic and cooking-oil industries. Palm trees are also 'tapped' two or three times daily for their sugar-rich sap – watching 'toddy tappers' shimmy up the notches in slender palm trunks to reach the thicket of stems at the top is one of Goa's defining sights. When fermented, the liquid is drunk as *todi*, which, like cashew juice, can also be distilled to make the potent hooch *feni* – the main cause of the fatal falls from palm trees recorded all too often in the Goan press.

One of Goa's grandest *palacios* stands just up the road from the church. **Sat Banzam Gor** (Seven Gables) sports an elaborate red-hued rococo façade with original oyster-shell windows and scrollwork picked out in whitewash. Built in 1790 by a private secretary to the Portuguese viceroy of Goa, it is still occupied by descendants of its original own-

Sat Banzam Gor

ers. Visits may be arranged through the local tourist office *(see page 126)*.

By comparison with the elegant piles in the colonial quarter, the 1950s municipal architecture of the bazaar area is decidedly unprepossessing, though the cavernous **covered market** at its heart, crammed with every kind of merchandise imaginable, is a great place for a wander. In the streets radiating from it, tea-traders, tailors and flower-sellers compete for custom amid heavy traffic. Since the recent completion of the Konkan Railway, providing a land link for Goa with Mumbai and the rest of coastal southwest India, Margao has received a huge influx of migrant workers from other states, and at rush hours feels as though it's buckling under the extra weight.

Inland from Margao

The well-watered countryside inland from Margao, separating the town from the Zuari River, was carved up in Portuguese times between the aristocratic Goan families who administered the colony. Many of their ancestral *palacios* still overlook the rice fields and wooded valleys of this picturesque area, and are well worth venturing from the coast to see. Only a couple actually open their doors to visitors, but no one will mind you admiring the others from beyond garden walls.

The back lanes of **Loutolim** village, 10km (6 miles) northeast of Margao, harbour a bumper crop of stately houses. The most famous, belonging to the Miranda family, stands just off the main square. Enclosed between a high wall and flanked by areca palms (source of the dynasty's betel nut fortune) dates from the early 18th century and is fronted by a splendid classical façade typical of the period. Its present incumbent, Maria João Carlos do Rosario de Brito de Miranda, is an acclaimed cartoonist.

A half-hour tour of another period house, the Casa Araujo Alvares, features as part of the **Ancestral Goa** exhibition (open daily 9am–6pm; admission fee), Loutolim's principal tourist attraction, where the centrepiece is a model village recreating scenes from life in the region a century or more ago.

Rice fields inland from Margao

A traditional Goan Catholic existence holds sway at nearby **Rachol**, where a seminary founded by the Jesuits in 1580 stands next to a church dedicated to the Order's founder, St Ignatius Loyola. Both buildings are in fine condition. India's first printing press was installed here in the 16th century by Thomas Stephens, the first Briton ever to set foot in India. In addition to relics of the former Roman emperor, St Constantine, the church houses a famous statue of

Antique furniture in the Menezes-Braganza wing

the Infant Jesus salvaged from a shipwreck on the coast of Africa and believed to possess miraculous powers. Outside, the course of a dry moat is the last vestige of the pre-colonial fort that once guarded the territory's eastern border.

Long before the Portuguese first sailed up the Konkan coast, the region was ruled from a city called Chandrapura, capital of the Kadambas, whose kingdom this was from the 6th century until the Vijayangar conquest of 1367–78. A few chunks of masonry and the ground plan of a temple are virtually all that survives of the once glittering capital, scattered around the outskirts of present-day **Chandor** village.

However, it's worth driving out here to see the wonderful **Perreira-Braganza/Menezes-Braganza house** – Goa's grandest stately home and one of the few geared up for visitors (open Mon–Sat 10am–noon, 3–6pm, Sun 3–6pm; entry by donation). Divided into two separate wings, the house is inhabited by descendants of different branches of the family

Sri Chandeshwar Temple

who originally built it on the site of their ancestral Hindu property in the 18th century. The east side (Perreira-Braganza) features a sumptuous Grand Salon, with crystal chandeliers, trompe-l'oeil murals and high-backed chairs given to the family by the King of Portugal. Pride of place in their old oratory is one of Goa's most precious relics, a diamond-encrusted fingernail of St Francis Xavier. Next door, the Menezes-Braganza wing belonged to a journalist, newspaper editor and freedom fighter who numbered among the few Goan aristocrats who openly opposed Portuguese rule. The interest here lies less in interior design than in the antique carved wood furniture, Chinese porcelain and books still carefully preserved alongside old family photos and portraits.

Just down the lane from the Menezes-Braganza mansion lies the more modest **Fernandes House** (open weekdays with prior appointment; tel: 278 4245), one of Goa's oldest *palacios*. Its present owner, Senhora Sarah Fernandes, shows visitors around the once opulent salons and bed-rooms on the first floor, and the hidden system of tunnels and trapdoors below where her ancestors used to hide from marauding bandits.

The other noteworthy stop in Margao's hinterland is the magical **Sri Chandeshwar Temple**, which surveys the serene landscape of south Goa from the top of the 370-m (1,214-ft) Chandranth Hill at **Parvath**. Hindu tradition dates the founding of the temple to a meteorite landing 2,500 years ago, but the present shrine, dedicated to Shiva in the form of Lord of the Moon, was built in the late 17th century. It en-closes a sanctuary hollowed from solid rock where the gold-en deity is flanked by stone statues of his consort Parvati and son Ganesh.

Usgalimal Rock Carvings

Etched out of a remote river bank deep in the Goan interior south of Chandor is a collection of prehistoric rock carvings, discovered only recently near the village of **Usgalimal**. They are believed to be between 10,000 and 20,000 years old, and comprise one of southern India's most enigmatic ancient sites. The figures mainly depict hunt-ing scenes – bulls, gazelles, antelope and bison with spears and arrows sticking in their flanks – although they also include some showing what look like human dancers and weird geometric shapes called 'triskelions'.

Finding the rock-art site can be difficult without the help of a guide or local person who knows its exact location. From Chandor, ask for directions to Rivona village, where you should be able to find some-one to show you the way. Flagged by a red-and-green Archaeological Survey signpost on the right side of the road, the carvings lie 16km (10 miles) south of Rivona, down a dirt track beyond some disused iron-ore workings.

Colva Beach

Ancient Hindu scriptures associate the creation of Goa with the sage Parasurama, Vishnu's sixth incarnation, who fired an arrow into the Arabian Sea from the Western Ghats, and was permitted by the gods to claim all the territory between him and the place it landed. The story is thought to be an echo of the period in the distant past when the Konkan coastal strip rose in height, and was subsequently drained, cleared and settled by Iron Age rice settlers (*parasuram* means axe in Sanskrit).

The exact spot where the sage's shaft allegedly fell to earth is identified in Hindu tradition as **Benaulim**, a Portuguese corruption of 'Banali' – 'The Arrow Place'. The present-day fishing and coconut village, now a fervently Christian settlement spread under a vast palm forest west of Margao, is the most congenial among a string of low-key resorts lining

Ice-cream hawker, Benaulim

25-km (15-mile) **Colva Beach**. Lying off the package tourist map, its small, family-run guest houses are frequented mainly by independent budget travellers taking time off from longer trips around India. Benaulim's great asset is the perfect swath of shell sand and surf that shimmers for miles in both directions from its beachfront. At the high-tide mark, rows of wooden outriggers sporting brightly painted bows stand against a backdrop of swaying palms and casuarina trees. Doze in the shade of one and you'll eventually be required to help its owners heave it into the sea.

Traditional coastal ways coexist more comfortably at Benaulim than they do in the next village north, **Colva**. This is a much more developed resort with beach that has become a bleak, litter-strewn expanse where bus parties pause for a noisy picnic and a paddle.

North of Colva, the paddy fields and palm groves behind the beach at **Majorda** and **Utorda** are punctuated at regular intervals by enormous five-star hotels, complete with elaborate swimming pools, lawns, air-conditioned gyms and palatial atrium lobbies. Their presence here owes as much to the proximity of the airport as the glorious beach on their doorstep, which curves north into the Dabolim Plateau, bristling with the pressure tanks and petrochemical stacks of south Goa's industrial zone.

Tucked away in a secluded fold of the Dabolim promontory, a stone's throw from the airport runway but well away from the nearby agro-fertiliser plant, is the resort of **Bogmalo**. The beach here, enfolded by a pair of low headlands, is dominated by an ugly high-rise hotel, but behind it the palm groves hide several small hotels and guest houses offering more traditional Goan hospitality.

More giant international resorts loom behind, in the dunes south of Colva and Benaulim, the largest concentration of them being at **Cavelossim** and neighbouring **Mobor**, where a sand spit brings the 25-km (15-mile) strand to an abrupt end. Air-conditioned shopping malls have sprung up along the road stringing together the holiday complexes, lending a slightly surreal air to what was, a little over a decade ago, a remote and inaccessible nook in the Goan coast. Wealthy Russian mafiosi and dot-com nouveaux riches from Bangalore, Hyderabad and Mumbai make up a large slice of the clientele who holiday here, alongside a dwindling contingent of north European charter tourists.

Cabo da Rama and Agonda

On the outskirts of Cavelossim, an old ferry chugs across the Assolna River towards **Assolna** village, a small crossroads bazaar surrounded by a belt of beautiful Portuguese *palacios* and rice fields. From here, the road south – the most scenic in all Goa – takes you through the ramshackle fishing centre of **Betul** before scaling a succession of laterite plateaux. In sharp contrast to the bleached savannah grass of the uplands, the hidden valleys dividing them are carpeted with lush palm forest, cashew groves, stands of areca and patches of viridescent paddy – perfect terrain for a back-road scooter ride.

You'll definitely need some form of transport to reach **Cabo da Rama** (Cape Rama), a rocky peninsula jutting into the Arabian Sea where the Hindu god Rama is believed to have sheltered during his mission to rescue wife Sita from clutches of the evil demon, Ravana, in Sri Lanka. Choked with weeds, tree roots and creepers, the battlements of an old fort crown the highest point of the headland. They were built by the Portuguese in 1763 on the site of a much older Hindu fort to protect against attack by Maratha and Dutch warships. Apart from the laterite walls and an impressive dry moat, a rusting cannon on the ramparts and a snug chapel inside are the only surviving vestiges of Portuguese rule. Wonderful views of this totally undeveloped stretch of coast extend in all directions.

It's well worth pressing on further south to reach **Agonda**, a Christian fishing village scattered behind a vast sandy beach. Tourist facilities here are, for the time being, rudimentary, limited to a handful of small guest houses, seafood restaurants and bamboo beach huts, but the wooded hills enfolding the bay form an undeniably exotic backdrop. The gradient of Agonda beach sometimes creates a dangerous undertow that makes swimming hazardous. Stick to the more sheltered, safer southern end, where the local fishing boats are moored.

Palolem and Beyond

Picturesque though it certainly is, Agonda serves as a mere prelude to the scenery awaiting you at **Palolem**, the next major beach south. Here, seams of the Sayadhri Hills rise straight from the sea, their base fringed by blackened boulders from which a beautiful arc of white sand curves away

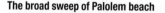

The broad sweep of Palolem beach

into a perfect bay, backed by coconut palms. It's not hard to see why this little slice of paradise has, over the last decade or so, become the prime destination for independent travellers to Goa. But Palolem has also become a victim of its own popularity. Despite laws forbidding construction less than 200m (220yds) away from the high-water mark, visitor numbers are overwhelming in peak season, causing water shortages and a horrendous build-up of plastic litter.

Oblivious to such problems – and the speed, and extent, of the village's dramatic metamorphosis in the 1990s – most tourists hole up for weeks, or months, in one of the many camps of palm-leaf huts behind Palolem beach. Forming an

Palolem palms

unbroken line next to them, a rank of brightly lit beach shacks service the sunbathers during the day and are the backbone of the village's nightlife after dark.

Apart from beach cricket, frisbee-throwing and body surfing, there's precious little to distract you from snoozing under the palm trees, unless you fancy an early-morning dolphin-spotting or fishing trip, or a walk at low tide to the magical island at the top of the beach.

For a change of scene, stroll south from Palolem and over the rocky headland to **Colom**, a scruffy Hindu fishing village with a travellers' scene based around a handful of cafés so laid back they and their clientele are virtually collapsing into the tiny sand bays in front.

From there, another five minutes' walk brings you to the next big beach, **Patnem**. Although it lacks the shade and sheltered water of Palolem, Patnem does host a string of pleasant little shacks and guest houses, some of them run by Europeans. The swimming is safe at most phases of the tide, though an undertow can spring up over full-moon periods.

After Patnem, the vision that lies in store on the far side of the next small headland south will come as a shock. Sprawling behind **Rajbag** beach, a vast new 'seven-star' luxury hotel complex – the Grand Resort Goa, part of the InterContinental chain – looks extremely out of place on this far-flung shoreline. It was completed in 2004, in spite of considerable local opposition, and looks set to herald a wave of major development ahead of the massive new naval base planned for Karwar, an hour's drive south in Karnataka.

The most southerly beach worth a mention in Goa lies on the far side of the Talpona River, which you can cross via a hand-paddled dug-out ferry from the end of Rajbag, or (more reliably) by heading 5km (3 miles) down NH-17 to the road bridge and turning west to follow the back road along the riverside. Here, remote and secluded **Galjibag**, a wild stretch of sand and dunes backed by casuarina trees, has virtually no visitors. Olive Ridley marine turtle nests are dotted along the sand, enclosed behind protective fences.

Mallikarjun Temple and Cotigao Wildlife Sanctuary

With so many exquisite beaches in the area, it can be hard to drag yourself away, though a couple of minor sights beyond Palolem deserve a foray inland. Signposted 6km (4 miles) down NH-17, the **Mallikarjun Temple** holds an ancient stone inner shrine with a brightly painted exterior that was renovated in the 18th century. Local Hindus come here to worship its presiding deity, Mallikarjun, a form of Shiva, and to consult the advice of oracles, or *kauls*, who take possession of the priests in trance ceremonies.

The other attraction in the area is the **Cotigao Wildlife Sanctuary**, 12km (7 miles) south of Palolem. Set up in the late 1960s, the park preserves just under 100 sq km (38 sq miles) of richly diverse woodland sheltering fragile populations of animals including jungle cats, gazelles, bears and hyenas – though don't expect to see any unless you're equipped to explore the innermost reaches of the reserve. Wardens at the Interpretative Centre, just off the main highway, collect admission fees and can supply maps and directions for viewing towers and waterholes.

EXCURSIONS FROM GOA

A couple of hours' train ride south of Goa on the Konkan Railway lies Gokarna, the sacred Hindu pilgrimage town par excellence, with a glorious coastline to complement the religious intensity of its temples. Gokarna was a major Shiva worship centre under the Vijayangar empire, the ruins of whose once resplendent city at Hampi, eight hours by rail east of Goa, rise from the foot of dry boulder hills and banana plantations, deep in the Deccan Plateau of central India. Both places are loaded with traditional Indian atmosphere, far from the modernity of the Goan coast.

Gokarna

Hindu pilgrimage centres in India often feel locked in a kind of time warp, little influenced by the trends and technologies transforming the rest of the country; **Gokarna** is no exception. Although only a two-hour train ride from Goa, the town remains staunchly old-fashioned both in appearance and traditions, seemingly oblivious to the tourism boom to the north.

Revered as a sacred site for hundreds, and maybe thousands, of years, it is believed to be where the evil demon Ravana dropped a powerful *lingam* he'd stolen from Shiva's holy abode on Mount Kailash in the Himalayas – an episode recounted in the epic *Ramayana*. On hitting the ground, the *Pranalingam* took root, and resides to this day in the soot-lined **Sri Mahabaleshwar Temple** in the dunes behind a broad sandy beach on the western edge of town. After a redemptive dip in the sacred surf, pilgrims file dripping wet through the shrine's central sanctuary for *darshan*, or ritual viewing of the deity, which Hindu lore claims possesses the power to absolve no less than 100 sins (including the most heinous of all, murder of a Brahmin priest).

Many other lesser temples cluster in the streets around Gokarna's bazaar. Wandering through the backstreets past wood-fronted houses and tiered terracotta roofs, you'll catch

Bathing *ghats* at Gokarna

Brahmins at Gokarna

glimpses through ancient doorways of scenes so time-less they might have jumped off the pages of medieval Sanskrit manuscripts: priests wrapped in cotton robes saying prayers on rosaries of *rudraksha* seeds; women in richly coloured saris threading marigolds into garlands by the light of oil lamps; and families sitting cross-legged on verandas eating *dal* and rice from dry banana leaves.

From the main town beach, a path leads south over a laterite headland to a series of wonderful beaches, the most famous being the **'Om' beach**, whose twin coves, separated by a rocky promontory, resemble the sacred Hindu *Om* symbol when viewed from the south. Fishing boats ferry tourists out to the more secluded bays colonised by camps of Western and Israeli hippies. Dirt roads are being bulldozed to some – harbingers of what must surely one day be full-scale development.

Hampi (Vijayangar)

The chaotic, polluted reality of contemporary India all too often falls short of the exotic visions depicted in holiday brochures and coffee-table books. But at **Hampi**, a ruined medieval city a day's journey inland from Goa, the clichés of the mystical East for once come alive: wild monkeys really do scamper over temple towers; dreadlocked sadhus, their foreheads smeared with ash and vermilion, pull yoga poses on the banks of a sacred river; and painted elephants bless pilgrims with their trunks as they file into incense-filled shrines.

Radiating around the modern village of Hampi, **Vijayangar**, the 'City of Victory', was in the 15th and 16th centuries the capital of India's last, and most powerful, Hindu empire – a metropolis of unparalleled wealth and sophistication. Vast riches from trade and tribute were channelled by its rulers into buildings that dazzled the few European travellers who ventured this far into the Indian interior. In 1520, the Portuguese explorer Domingo Pães wrote in awe of the city's glittering festivals and bazaars groaning with gold and jewels.

Only 45 years after Pães's visit, however, Vijayangar was destroyed in an act of military vengeance more destructive than any other seen on the subcontinent. The Hindu empire had evolved as a response to the expansion across the Deccan of Muslim invaders from the northwest, who eventually formed a belt of sultanates from coast to coast. As long as these kingdoms feuded and squabbled, the Hindu lands to

Hampi: Virupaksha Temple from Hemakuta

> Accommodation in
> Hampi is limited to a
> handful of basic budget
> lodges. The nearest
> hotels offering Western-
> standard amenities and
> comforts are located in
> the railway town of
> Hospet, 13km (8 miles)
> southwest of Hampi.

the south were secure, protected by the might of Vijayangar's army. But in 1565
they finally buried their dif-
ferences long enough to
wage a decisive attack. During and after the appalling
Battle of Talikota, Vijayangar's exquisite monuments
were reduced to rubble. Yet,
today, the ornately carved
masonry and crumbling temple towers, set against the boulder hills and banana plantations of the Tungabadhra River,
continue to cast an extraordinary spell.

Exploring the Ruins

The ruins are scattered over a total area of nearly 30 sq km
(11 sq miles), but the most important monuments resolve
into two distinct groups. The first, around the main street of
Hampi bazaar, is dominated by the gigantic **Virupaksha
Temple** (open daily 8am–12.30pm, 3–6.30pm; admission
fee), whose mighty *gopura* tower can be seen for miles in
every direction.

From Virupaksha, either stroll down the sacred ford and
riverside *ghats* to watch the pilgrims taking their holy dip, or
walk east along the bazaar and beyond, passing a string of
carved stone shrines, to the beautiful **Vitthala Temple** (open
daily 8am–4pm; admission fee). This UNESCO-listed monu-
ment is famed for its pillars, ornately sculpted in the form of
rampant horses – the principal source of the Vijayangar empire's wealth. Near by, coracle men, or *putti-wallahs*, wait to
paddle passengers to the far banks of the Tungabhadra, from
where sandy tracks thread through the fields to villages hidden in the banana groves.

A 3-km (2-mile) swath of greenery separates this northern group of monuments from the grander southern one, which centres on the **Royal Enclosure** (open daily 8am–4pm; admission fees for individual sites). A sprawl of temples, bath complexes, domed elephant stables, pleasure palaces and ceremonial platforms, the area is elaborately decorated with mythological bas-reliefs and enclosed by colossal granite battlements. In a couple of days, you can't hope to do much more than scratch the surface of Hampi's archaeological treasures. But don't let this deter you. The site's great appeal lies less in ticking off its monuments than in its unique atmosphere: the other-worldly boulder landscapes, the serenity of the river and the magical sunsets, which infuse everything with an amazing golden light.

Carved pillars at Hampi's Vitthala temple

That said, two sights should not, under any circumstances, be skipped. The first is the view at dawn from the top of **Matanga Hill**, as the sun rises above the mystical Tiruvengalatha Temple. The second is the spellbinding panorama at sunset from the Hanuman, or **'Monkey' Temple**, an hour or so's walk north from the far side of the river, where an escarpment falls away to one of the most wondrous landscapes you'll ever set eyes on.

WHAT TO DO

No matter how much you enjoy lounging on the beach, you're bound at some stage to want a break from the relentless Goan sun and surf. A fleet of mini-van taxis are on hand to whisk visitors away on sightseeing (*see page 123*) and shopping trips, while the more culturally adventurous can revive sun-weary bodies with a traditional ayurvedic massage or yoga session. Nightlife in the state is far less full-on than many people expect (raves being a real rarity these days), but there is no shortage of clubs and bars in the resorts, and beach shacks usually stay open until the last customer staggers home. Finally, activities guaranteed to blow away the cobwebs after a night out include parascending from the clifftops in north Goa, kite-surfing in the stiff breezes and scuba diving around the offshore islands.

SHOPPING

Indians regard Goa as an expensive destination, but coming from more developed parts of the world you might be surprised by how little souvenirs and other shop goods cost. Traders, at least those in the resorts, are well aware of this, of course, and may well try to take advantage of your ignorance by asking prices way above the norm – which is why you should be prepared to haggle.

Where and How to Shop

The Anjuna flea market and Ingo's Night Market at Arpora are Goa's two tourist shopping hotspots, held on Wednesdays and Saturday evenings respectively. In both cases, bargaining is

Shoes at Anjuna flea market

Beach stalls at Palolem

very much the order of the day: it's not unusual to be asked 10 or more times what the trader will accept as their 'last price' (quite simply because some naive foreigners aren't aware of the 'system' and will hand over what they're initially asked for).

Goa's main towns – Panjim, Mapusa and Margao – are crammed with more conventional shops. As a rule of thumb, expect general stores and fancy, air-conditioned boutiques to offer genuinely 'fixed prices'; rates at other places, especially clothes shops and stalls, will most definitely be negotiable, though quite to what extent is a matter of experience. When in doubt, just ask 'Fixed price?' and gauge the shopkeeper's reaction.

What to Buy

Flimsy cotton **clothes** for flopping around the beach in – baggy shorts, loose shirts, pyjamas and sarongs – are sold at knock-down prices from stalls in all the resorts, usually by Lamani 'gypsy' women from Karnataka. When they can stay one step ahead of the local cops, their younger sisters and daughters illegally hawk the same stuff in huge bundles on the beach.

For better quality, more formal or Western wear, you can either shop in the towns (Panjim is best for men's boxed shirts and labels such as Benetton and Levi's), or else buy the cloth separately and have it made to measure – bring along your favourite clothes for the local tailors to copy.

Polycotton dominates **textile** shops in the town markets, but at government-run Khadi Gramodyog stores in Panjim and Margao, hand-spun silk and pure Indian cotton are sold by the metre, often at unbelievably low prices (with extra discounts over *Diwali* and during October).

Handicrafts account for the bulk of the glass-fronted boutiques in the resorts, most of which are run by Kashmiris – the wiliest of all Goa's traders. Ranging from Rs50 papier-maché baubles to $1,000 carpets, their stock tends to vary greatly in price and quality. Basically, unless you're 100 percent sure

---

Lifestyle Stores

At the opposite end of the shopping spectrum from Goa's beach hawkers are the so-called 'lifestyle stores' dotted around the state. Set up in elegant old Portuguese-era *palacios*, these swish boutiques assemble desirable merchandise such as traditional Goan wood furniture, expensive silks, designer clothes, antique statues and other objets d'art, hand-picked from regions all over the country. Prices, it has to be said, are astronomical by Indian standards, although comparable with what you'd expect to pay for similar goods at home – and the shopping experience itself is very laid back. Unlike in most Goan souvenir emporia, you're usually left to browse in peace.

Goa's original, and best, lifestyle store is **Sangolda**, 4km (2¹/₂ miles) east of Calangute on the CHOGM Road to Porvorim. Next door, **Saudades** is in a similar mould. For Portuguese-flavoured items, including *azulejos* (painted tiles) and old-style planters' chairs, and floaty designer cotton garments, try **Cocoon**, midway between Calangute and Baga. On the road to Old Goa at Ribandar, **Camelot** is also good for local designer wear, and **Manthan**, near Benaulim in south Goa, sells contemporary art, books and fine-quality handicrafts.

One of the few authentic Goan souvenirs you could take home are bags of top-quality, export-grade cashew nuts. The best places to buy them are the specialist shops, such as Zantye's, on Panjim's main shopping street, 18 June Road.

you can tell the difference between a fake and genuine pashmina shawl, or a top-grade Persian rug from a copy, stick to the more humble Indian souvenirs: wooden religious statues, Buddhist *thangkas* and Rajasthani miniature paintings.

Himalayan curios and **silver jewellery**, inlaid with semi-precious stones such as turquoise, coral, carnelian or lapis lazuli, are the speciality of Tibetan traders (although Kashmiris also dabble in this field). Silver items are always weighed before being priced, but this is really just showmanship and a prelude to the usual round of protracted haggling. Tibetans are less prone to chicanery than their Kashmiri cousins; they're also hard to budge when it comes to price.

NIGHTLIFE

At one time Goa was almost a byword for drug-fuelled beach parties, and lots of people still come expecting to find a wild nightlife, only to be disappointed by what ranks as a fairly tame scene by Western standards. Even so, more and more clubs open each season, and with liquor laws more liberal (and drink prices lower) than anywhere else in the country, the state's bars and beach shacks do a roaring trade after dark. More sober alternatives to the many booze-based entertainments on offer include recitals of classical Indian music and ritual theatre. And if all else fails, there always Bollywood…

Nightclubs

In India, the very notion of men and women dancing together in public (outside family weddings) is still a novelty reserved for the sons and daughters of only the most Western-ised elite in major cities. The normal rules tend not to apply in Goa, where the nightlife has always been a step ahead of the rest of the country, but clubs are still few and far between.

Live bands are a feature of Ingo's Night Market on Saturday evenings at Arpora, north Goa, which cranks up into party mode around 10pm. Admission is free.

Until recently, only one spot was worthy of being called a club. Spilling down the sides of a dune behind Baga beach, **Tito's** started out life as a tourist hang-out, but over the years gained a nationwide profile that attracted streams of mostly male revellers from other states, lured by reports of scantily clad foreign women (and all that implied). The club still tends to be male-dominated, but the rowdy element that

Ingo's Night Market at Arpora

made it a no-go zone for self-respecting women during the late 1990s has been held in check, and a more relaxed vibe now prevails.

Tito's main rival, **Cuba Cubana**, on a hilltop above Arpora, is an altogether smoother set up, such as you'd expect to find in a Mediterranean resort, with an open-air dance floor, a plunge pool and chill-out areas scattered over garden terraces. Both it and Tito's operate door policies that favour women: 'ladies' get in free on most nights, and couples pay

Under the Moon

Beach parties have been a feature of life in north Goa's coastal villages since the hippy days of the 1970s, when bands and DJs would turn up on full-moon nights to play for crowds of stoned tourists. By the end of the 1980s, the replacement of LSD with ecstasy as the dancer's drug of choice not only had a dramatic impact on the kind of music being played at these events, but also transformed the impromptu revelries into full-scale, well-organised raves for thousands of people.

At the peak of the party wave in the early 1990s, the thump of techno and trance music formed an almost constant nocturnal soundtrack for the unfortunate inhabitants of Anjuna and Vagator. Paid off with bribes, the Goan police would turn a blind eye (or a deaf ear) to the mini-festivals. But opposition from disgruntled locals steadily grew, and finally erupted ahead of the millennium celebrations in 2000, when a Mapusa-based environmental group managed to get the High Court to impose a ban on amplified music after 10pm.

Since then, proper full-moon parties have tended to feature only over Christmas and New Year, if at all. The dance scene, meanwhile, has shifted to permanent venues: Club Paradiso in Anjuna and the Nine Bar at Ozran Vagator, whose hefty sound systems pump out Goan trance on dance floors decorated with fluoro-painted Hindu deities.

less than do two 'unaccompanied' single men (or 'stags', as they're called).

Further north up the coast, **Club Paradiso** in Anjuna and the **Nine Bar** at Ozran Vagator offer a less conventional kind of dance experience. In the absence of regular raves, they've become the hubs of Goa's techno and trance scenes, drawing a druggier, alternative clientele – many of them young Israelis.

Bars

For most visitors, nightlife in Goa usually consists of a leisurely restaurant meal followed up by an extended session at one of the count-

'Rave trees' painted for the full moon, Kerim beach

less bars competing for custom in the resorts. These range from rough-and-ready beach shacks serving not-so-cold beer by the bottle, to hip 'lounge bars' where you can order imported scotch and gastro tapas while listening to DJs playing whatever's currently cool in Amsterdam or Paris.

Along the main strip in Baga, you'll also come across the inevitable Brit-orientated 'pubs' boasting wide-screen sports TV, as well as full-on karaoke and cocktail bars. The most consistently lively late-night watering hole, however, has to be **Mambo's** – a beachside extension of Tito's, just below the main club venue. For a more sophisiticated vibe, try **Congo**, on the southern (Sinquerim) side of Candolim's

CHOGM Road, an ultra-trendy bar patronised by loaded media and dot-com types from Bangalore and Mumbai.

Cinema

Goa hosted the prestigious International Film Festival of India in 2004 and 2005, and looks set to become the event's permanent venue. One of the major benefits to the state of holding the week-long festival has been the appearance in Panjim of a state-of-the-art multiplex cinema, the **Inox** (<www.inoxmovies.com>). At least a couple of foreign-language films – usually Hollywood blockbusters – are screened here at any given time. But the real crowd-pullers tend to be the latest offerings from Bollywood. Tickets can be purchased in advance at the box office or on the night.

SPORTS

Reflecting the state's Portuguese heritage, **soccer** is Goa's most popular sport. You'll see it played everywhere, from knockabouts on the beach to more organised local league games on dirt pitches that double as paddy fields in the rainy season. Goa also has several of the country's top professional sides, with half a dozen teams in the National Football League (NFL). The official NFL soccer season lasts from the middle of January until mid-May, with the big matches reserved for the enormous Nehru Stadium in Margao.

Goa's **cricket** sides don't enjoy the same high profile

> Boat trips, for early-morning dolphin-spotting or fishing, are a popular option. They vary in length and levels of comfort, but are invariably enjoyable. As with all pre-arranged trips, always check in advance whether meals and bottled water are included in the price, and that life jackets and adequate shade are provided.

as do the soccer teams, but the game is played with great gusto by local boys on the beaches, where as a tourist you'll be welcome to join in. The same applies to volleyball, which Goan lads – and the Nepalis who work as cooks and waiters in the restaurants – love to play during the late afternoon.

Otherwise, the only sports on offer in Goa are more adventurous activities. Up in Aswem in north Goa, a team of Swiss and Geman **kite-surfing** enthusiasts hire out equipment and offer tuition. The onshore breezes that blow most afternoons are ideal for beginners.

Parascending, where you fly a manoeuverable parachute using thermal updrafts from clifftops, is another adventure sport that's fast becoming a feature of beach life in the north of the state. Instructors can be contacted at Anjuna (on the cliffs at the southern side of the beach) and Arambol (based at the Relax Inn restaurant on the beach). It's worth remembering that parascending can be dangerous (a tourist died in Anjuna in 2001 after crashing on a tandem flight with his instructor), and that it might not be covered by your insurance policy. A less risky alternative is parasailing, where you're hauled into the sky from the sea by a speedboat: Baga and Calangute are the beaches for this.

Beach volleyball

Goa isn't exactly a **diving** hotspot – the silt that pours onto the coast in the state's many rivers ensures the sea is murky and visibility poor – but one established, expat-run outfit uses a powerboat to reach islands and underwater plateaux four hours away where conditions are world class. Based at Bogmalo, near the airport in south Goa, Goa Diving (<www.goadiving.com>) offers training for PADI courses as well as excursions for qualified divers.

HOLISTIC THERAPIES

A beach holiday in Goa can be a great rejuvenator, especially if you combine it with one or more of the holistic therapies that are widely available in the resorts.

Oil for ayurvedic treatment

Ayurveda, India's system of traditional medicine, can involve anything from a basic restorative massage using aromatic oils to a full-scale course of treatment of herbs for specific ailments or disorders. As a visitor, your initial problem will be finding a dependable, qualified practitioner. Anyone can set up shop as an 'ayurvedic doctor', but only those with certificates from Indian medical institutes are likely to do you any good. If in any doubt, either stick to the health spas in the five-star hotels, or call at the Ayurvedic Natural Health Centre (ANHC) in Saligao,

5km (3 miles) inland from Calangute, where the full range of different treatments are offered by trained practitioners.

The ANHC also offers courses in **yoga**, India's other great contribution to the health and well-being of the world. There's no better way to consolidate the beneficial effects of sunshine, sea water and fresh air on your body than an early-morning 'salute to the sun', or *surya namaskar*, though, once again, you could do yourself more harm than good by following guidance from someone under-qualified.

Yoga comes in various forms. The main distinction to bear in mind is between the styles developed by Pune-based yoga master, Sri B.K.S. Iyengar, and in Mysore by Sri K. Pattabhi Jois. Whereas Iyengar yoga tends to favour static poses, with the use of props and apparatus to help you maintain the correct position, Ashtanga yoga is more dynamic and aerobic – you literally jump between poses (not recommended for anyone with back or any other orthopaedic problems).

Yoga Centres in Goa

In addition to the yoga instructors attached to most 'health spas' in five-star hotels, the following yoga teachers and schools in Goa offer expert tuition:

Himalayan Iyengar Yoga Centre, Arambol beach, Pernem, <www.hiyogacentre.com>.
Maggie Hughes, 1277 Anna Vaddo, Candolim, tel: 9226 367895, <www.yogamaggieh.com>.
Purple Valley, Granpa's Inn, Gaun Waddo, Anjuna, tel: 227 3270, <www.yogagoa.com>.

CHILDREN'S GOA

With acres of sand and shallow water on your doorstep, you shouldn't have too much trouble occupying any children you might have in tow. Swimming is generally safe – though be warned that at certain phases of the tide some beaches can develop nasty undertows that will sweep little ones off their feet in seconds. Jellyfish are another hazard: they generally stick to water at least 2m (6ft) deep, but also get hauled up with fishing nets and dumped on the sand, where they can still sting unprotected feet. Other dangers to keep in mind are dogs – which might not all be as cute as they look, with rabies an ever-present threat – and, of course, the sun, which from first light will be too strong for fair-skinned tots, even in December and January.

Dedicated child-friendly activities are all but non-existent in Goa, but most kids will enjoy dolphin-spotting boat rides, while at the flea markets they can expect to come face to face with a tame elephant or two and other animals. In addition, the Inox cinema in Panjim generally screens kids' movies from the US.

Diwali star

Festivals and Events

6 January: *Festa dos Reis*. Epiphany celebration, during which young boys dressed as the Three Kings ride to chapel on white horses.

January: *Shantadurga* festival, Goa's main Hindu temple festival, also known as the Procession of the Umbrellas because it is led by 12 colourful umbrellas carried on poles by lads smeared in red powder.

February–March: Carnival. Three days of madness and parades focusing around Panjim. *Shigmo*. Goa's version of the Hindu Holi spring festival includes processions of floats and the usual throwing of paint bombs – so don't go out in your Sunday best.

March–April: Easter. Celebrated with fasting, feasting and High Mass. Procession of the Saints. Life-size effigies of 26 Christian saints and martyrs are paraded around Old Goa (near Panjim) on the first Monday of Easter week.

May: *Igitun Chalne*. Famous fire-walking ritual in which devotees of the goddess Lairaya enter trances and walk over hot coals.

June: *Sanjuan*. The feast day of St John, celebrated with particular enthusiasm by the Christians of Arambol. *Sangodd*. The feast day of St Peter, the patron saint of fishers. Traditional dramas, or *khells*, are performed on stages made from boats.

September–October: *Dusshera*. Major Hindu festival that celebrates Rama's victory over Ravana in the *Ramayana*, and the goddess Durga's over the buffalo-headed. Effigies are burned and school kids perform ritual plays.

October–November: *Diwali*. Hindu 'festival of lights' to celebrate Rama and Sita's homecoming.

November–December: International Film Festival of India. Goa's answer to Cannes, hosted by Panjim.

3 December: Feast of St Francis Xavier. Tens of thousands worship at the tomb of SFX in Old Goa.

24–5 December: Christmas. *Missa de Galo*, Midnight Mass (literally 'Cockerel Mass'), marks the start of Goa's most important Christian festival. Tourist ravers party in Anjuna, police permitting.

EATING OUT

Eating out, whether at a simple palm-leaf shack on the beach or a fancy gourmet restaurant in a five-star hotel, is one of the great pleasures of visiting Goa. Among the legacies of the state's cosmopolitan past is a cuisine heavily influenced by Portuguese culinary traditions, but prepared with a typically south Indian relish for hot spices. It was the Portuguese who first introduced the chilli to India, and Goans have elevated its use to an art form. Fiery fish curry and rice is the mainstay of the local diet. The tourist's staple meal, on the other hand, tends to be a steak of succulent grilled fish dished up with potato chips and tomato salad, and an ice-cold bottle of Kingfisher beer.

Simple fare such as this, despite the hike in seafood prices caused by the tourist boom, is inexpensive by Western standards. Even a meal at one of the state's swankier restaurants shouldn't set you back much more than Rs500 (£7) per head – unless you splash out on the imported wines that have become fashionable additions to upscale menus in recent years.

Mapusa, the principal town of north Goa, hosts a wonderful fresh-produce market each Friday morning. Along with a bewildering array of fruit, veg and flowers from local gardens, this is where you'll find authentically Goan delicacies such as *chouriço* sausages, cashew *feni* and scrumptious traditional cakes and coconut biscuits *(see page 51)*.

Goan Food

Over four-and-a-half centuries of colonial rule, Goans developed their own highly original brand of cuisine, drawing on both the traditions of the Konkan coast and tastes and ingredients

Chouriço **sausages at Mapusa market**

imported by the Portuguese. The results are often as quirky as Goa's idiosyncratic architecture. A typically hybrid example, and the state's most famous culinary export, is vindaloo (from the Portuguese *vinho*, meaning wine, and *alho*, garlic), a hot, spicy and sour sauce traditionally served with pork.

Christian and Hindu communities have their own particular takes on most standard dishes. But neither are easy to find in restaurants, for the simple reason that, first and foremost, traditional Goan food is a family affair, prepared by women for home consumption. Few professional chefs can afford the time local housewives lavish on hand-grinding coconut and spices to produce their subtle curries. As a consequence, local cooking keeps a low profile in the resorts. To sample definitive regional dishes, you either have to be invited to eat with a Goan family, or know where to look.

The key element of every Goan meal, whether Christian or Hindu, vegetarian or non-veg, is the *masala* (*mirem* in

Rich and colourful spices

Konkani): a gravy or sauce made from a complicated mixture of spices and condiments. Different kinds of fish, meat or vegetables require different *masalas*, but they all tend to be derived from a common base of shredded coconut, coconut milk, onions, palm vinegar, tamarind, garlic, ginger, coriander, cumin, cardamom, cloves and, of course, hot chillies (the punchiest varieties of which tend to come from Kashmir). The effect is at once sour, tangy, bitter and pungent – and a revelation if you are only used to the oily, sweetened sauces served in Western curry houses.

A red, chilli-rich paste called *rechead* forms the basis of Goan fish curry, eaten twice each day by most working Goans with a mound of fluffy white rice and slices of millet-fried mackerel. Eye-wateringly hot, the meal is something of an acquired taste, but one well worth sampling at some stage during your holiday. *Rechead* is also used extensively with all kinds of seafood, smeared on the insides of steamed or fried pomfret or spread over calamari and fish steaks.

Other classic Goan seafood preparations include fish *caldin* (boneless steaks of white fish such as snapper or barramundi cooked in a gravy of coconut milk, curry leaves and sour kokum fruit) and *ambot tik*, literally 'hot and sour' (shark, mackerel or eel simmered in red chilli, tamarind and vinegar). Clams (*tisreo* in Konkani) are also eaten loaded with coconut and spices. Wander along the banks of a large estuary or mudflat at low tide and you'll sometimes see whole villages immersed up to their necks in water collecting them to make scrumptious *tisreo masala*.

While Hindus are strictly forbidden from eating **beef** (in fact, most kinds of meat), and Muslims abstain from **pork**, Goan Catholics eat both as often as possible. On important feast days (such as Christmas), a pig will typically be slaughtered to make *sorpotel,* a rich stew made from kidneys, liver and sweetbreads. **Chicken** is more likely to be prepared as a *xacuti*, steeped in an ultra-hot blend of spices and coconut milk that was originally made as a restorative for paddy workers during the monsoon planting season. Both can be accompanied by plain rice, or more satisfyingly with *sanna* – steamed rice cakes flavoured with partly fermented palm sap (*todi*).

In addition to the Portuguese predilection for meat, Goan Catholics inherited from their former rulers a great love of breads, cakes and puddings. **Bakeries** are still a real feature of life all across the state. One of the definitive sounds of Goan villages is the honk of the *poee*-seller's bicycle horn as he does his round dispensing fluffy white *poee* rolls from a basket strapped to the back of his bike. *Dodol*, a sticky,

Bhaji-Pao – the Goan Breakfast

The dish with which the majority of Goans kickstart their day is a small plate of spicy stew made from coconut and green peas, laced with hot chillies and pepper. Into this helping of *bhaji* is dunked a Goan bread roll (*pao* or *poee*), washed down with a glass of strong, sweet tea or coffee. You'll find tiny stalls and cafés selling *bhaji-pao* breakfasts in all the main towns and marketplaces.

gelatinous sweet boiled down from industrial quantities of coconut milk and crystallised sugar-cane juice *(jaggery)*, is reserved for special occasions, such as the return or departure of a relative from overseas. The other dessert guaranteed to give an expatriate Goan homesickness is *bebinca* (*bibik* in Konkani), a seven-layered cake made of eggs, coconut milk and *jaggery*, slow baked and saturated in custard.

Finding authentic Goan food is less straightforward than you'd imagine. Only a handful of restaurants around the state serve meals that compare with what locals eat at home. These include: Viva Panjim! in Panjim; Florentine's, in Saligao, just inland from Calangute in north Goa; the legendary Martin's Corner in Betalbatim, near Colva and Durigo's, near Benaulim, both in south Goa. *(See Listings starting on page 136.)*

Tourist Fare

When tourists first started to come to Goa in numbers back in the 1980s, local fishing families were quick to adapt their local cooking styles to accommodate more sensitive foreign palates. At makeshift palm-leaf structures on the beaches, they'd knock up **grilled fish** – kingfish, pomfret, tuna or tiger prawns – in tasty butter-garlic sauce, with chips and a salad made from tomato, grated cabbage, coriander and lemon juice. Simple, fresh and delicious, this exotic version of old-fashioned fish and chips remains the basic tourist fare, served at countless shacks up and down the state. Menus grow more and more ambitious with each season, but you'll rarely eat a more mouth-watering meal than a plate of whatever's come straight from the fish market or local boats.

Away from the beaches, the resorts are crammed with much fancier restaurants offering cuisine from all over India and the rest of the world. Authentic **Italian** pizza and pasta are currently very much in vogue, and you'll also find a sprinkling of sophisticated **Thai** and **French** establishments.

Kingfish ready for grilling

South Indian

For a quick, inexpensive, delicious sit-down meal or snack in one of Goa's towns, your best option will be a local *udipi*, or south Indian canteen – named after the Hindu pilgrimage town of Udipi in southern Karnataka, where many of the dishes originated. Simple, basic places, *udipis* are staffed by a team of kitchen boys in cotton overalls alongside smarter waiters. They are nearly always scrupulously vegetarian (which means no eggs or fish as well as no meat).

At **lunchtime** *udipis* provide a vast array of set *thalis* consisting of half a dozen different spicy vegetable dishes and lentil stews *(dals)*, accompanied by rice, poppadoms, yogurt *raita* and a serving of pickle *(achar)* and *chatnis*, all placed in stainless-steel cups and put on a large round tin tray (called a *thali*). The boys walk around the canteen spooning more on to diners' plates as they eat.

For **breakfast** and throughout the day, *udipis* also serve steamed rice cakes, or *idlys*, with deep-fried, round *wada* doughnuts made from maize flour. These are served with small helpings of coconut-based *chatni* and a tangy, hot lentil sauce flavoured with tamarind, called *sambar*.

Chatni-sambar is also the standard accompaniment for the most famous of all *udipi* snacks, the *dosa* – huge, circular pancakes made from fermented rice-flour batter fried on a hot griddle plate and rolled into a huge tube. When stuffed with a mix of potato, onions, chopped green chillies, pieces of coconut and mustard seeds, it becomes a more substantial *masala dosa* – a wonderfully tasty meal in itself. No two will ever be the same, and every joint has its particular style of preparation. *Dosas* can come with a variety of fillings, a drizzle of *ghee* (clarified butter), wafer-thin or thick. The batter may also be blended with finely chopped onions and poured in cross-hatched diagonal lines onto the griddle, rather than spread into a round pancake, to make a crunchier *rawa masala dosa*.

North Indian: Mughlai

From the opposite side of India, **Mughlai** cuisine – the gastronomic offshoot of north Indian cooking – takes its cue from the elaborate culinary styles favoured by the Moghul emperors. The intermingling of Hindu India's love of spices with the Persian and Afghan invaders' predilection for saffron, nuts and dried fruit gave rise to dishes famed for their delicate flavours and rich sauces. Chicken and mutton form the basis of most of them, but fresh vegetables and pulses are also extensively used.

Mughlai cooking also gave the world the *tandoor* clay oven, used to quick-bake the kind of kebabs, *tikka* and *naan* breads enjoyed in curry houses in the West – only in Goa they're deployed to considerably greater effect by *tandoori* chefs to bake whole fish as well as lamb and chicken, using coatings of spice pastes and superb yogurt-based sauces.

Drinks

Goa's licensing laws are the most liberal in India, and alcohol is very much a part of life in the state – although one that brings with it considerable problems and hardships. Distilled from palm sap or the juice of cashew fruits, *feni*, the local tipple, makes alcoholics of many of the local men who produce it. *Feni*-induced falls from trees and sclerosis of the liver are two of the most common causes of death in coastal villages.

Around the resorts, Goa's own Kingfisher **beer** really is (as its slogan claims) 'The King of Good Times', consumed in prodigious quantities by visitors and locals alike. It tastes much better straight from a refrigerator than off the blocks of ice where bottles tend to be stored at beach shacks, and is much less glycerated than rival brands (Indian manufacturers lace their beers with glycerin as a preservative).

Cashews and *feni*

Whisky, rum, vodka and other **spirits** are also ubiquitous, though internationally recognisable labels are made under licence in India and may not taste the same as they do at home.

Wine, imported to Goa since the very earliest colonial times, is still quite a luxury. With viticulture now firmly established in the nearby Western Ghat mountains, output and quality of both whites and reds are increasing year on year, but prices are high by Indian standards, and the finished products rarely comparable with an average supermarket wine you might buy at home. While restaurants will typically mark up a bottle of wine by at least 100 percent, you'll find the same stock sold for half the price at liquor stores all over the state. Brands to look out for include Sula, Grovers and Château Indage.

A popular thirst-quencher

Available at every street corner and beach shack, Coca-Cola, Pepsi and 7Up dominate Goa's **soft drinks** market, but you will never be far away from healthier alternatives that will quench your thirst much more effectively. Freshly squeezed orange and pine-apple juice, milkshakes and *lassis* (a cooling blend of sweetened milk and yogurt) feature on most café menus and are deliciously refreshing. However, before you order, make sure your drink comes with 'no ice' (this is likely to have been made from untreated tap water, unless otherwise stated).

To Help You Order...

menu please	**matso menu di**	thank you	**dio boray korunc**
bill please	**matxem bill di**	not spicy	**maka tik naka**
water	**oodak**	spoon	**chomcho**
no ice	**barf naka**	fork	**garf**
tea	**chai**	knife	**suri**

...and Read the Menu

Breads (Roti)
chapati	flat, unleavened bread
masala dosa	crispy pancake made from lentil flour
poee/pao	bread rolls
puri	deep-fried and puffed-up wheat bread
sanna	steamed rice pikelets
uttapam	moist, savoury rice-flour pancake

Meat
leitao	suckling piglet
sorpotel	pickled pork in spicy sauce

Seafood
bangra	mackerel	**mori**	shark
chonok	barramundi	**paloo**	bream
eison	kingfish	**pomflit**	pomfret
gobro	rockfish	**shenanio**	mussels
kooli	crab	**sultan**	tiger prawns
modso	lemon fish	**tamoso**	snapper

Fruit (Foll) *and Nuts*
adzar	tender coconut	**kazu**	cashew
ambo	mango	**laranj**	orange
ananas	pineapple	**narl**	coconut

HANDY TRAVEL TIPS

An A–Z Summary of Practical Information

A

ACCOMMODATION (See also the list of RECOMMENDED HOTELS starting on page 128)

Independent travellers, whether arriving from abroad or other Indian states, should arrange at least the first few nights' accommodation a fortnight or more in advance. Pressure on beds is most intense over Christmas and New Year, when room rates typically double or triple in price. At other times, you can expect to find a decent, clean place to stay with a fan and en-suite bathroom from Rs250 (£3.50/US$2) per night. Tariffs, particularly at the lower end of the scale, are never as rigidly fixed as they might seem, fluctuating with demand, and if you intend to check in somewhere for more than four or five nights it's always worth trying to negotiate a discount.

Foreigners arriving at a hotel or guest house will have to fill out a 'C Form' listing their passport and visa details. The hotel owner has to submit this to the local police station within 48 hours. Bills are usually settled in cash, though debit and credit cards are accepted by five-star hotels and most upscale places.

AIRPORT

Goa's airport, Dabolim, lies 30km (18 miles) south of the capital, Panjim – roughly an hour's drive from the main package-tourist belt at Calangute, or 20–45 minutes from the resorts of south Goa. Arrival formalities can be frustratingly slow. Count on at least an hour to clear passport control, baggage reclaim and customs, and keep close tabs on any paperwork you fill out: a piece torn off your arrival form and given to you at the passport desk has to be handed over at the customs gate later (without it you won't be allowed to leave).

Porters can be a real nuisance, attempting to make you pay for free luggage trolleys. Another scam to watch out for is crooked money changers at the currency desks: check the exchange rates, transaction charges and calculations very carefully before leaving the counter.

Taxis queue outside the main concourse. Purchase a ticket to your chosen destination from the **Pre-Paid Taxi Booth** facing the main exit (prices are on a wallchart), and hand over the chit to your driver.

Airport enquiries: tel: 254 0806.

B

BUDGETING FOR YOUR TRIP

Goa is inexpensive by international standards, and foreign currency can go a lot further than it does in most holiday destinations. Conversely, coming from other Indian states you'll find it more expensive, especially in the resorts.

After accommodation, transport is likely to prove your main expense. When renting a taxi and driver for sightseeing excursions, it's a good idea to get together with other tourists and split the fare:

Airport transfer. Taxi from the airport to Panjim, 30km (18 miles) Rs450 (£5.75/US$10).

Accommodation. Room in mid-range hotel, per night (including all taxes) Rs800 (£10/US$18).

Meals and drinks. Breakfast in your hotel Rs150 (£2/US$3.50); light lunch in a south Indian café Rs75 (£1/US$1.70); dinner at an expensive restaurant Rs750 (£10/US$17); fish supper at a beach shack with drinks Rs350 (£4.50/US$8); beer (650ml bottle) Rs75 (£1/US$1.70); bottled water Rs15 (20p/US$0.34).

Excursions. To Dudhsagar Falls or Old Goa/Ponda temples Rs1,200 (£15/US$26.50). Dolphin-spotting cruise Rs550 (£7/US$12.50).

C

CAR AND MOTORCYCLE HIRE (RENTAL)

Self-drive – available from companies such as Sai Service (tel: 241 7478 or 241 7055, <www.saiservice.com>) and Hertz (<www.hertz.

com>) – is an expensive rarity in Goa. For sightseeing and shopping trips, it invariably works out cheaper to book a taxi and driver *(see page 123)*, which also allows you leave the often terrifying idiosyncrasies of Goa's roads to an expert. Alternatively, consider renting a two-wheeler. Your hotel will help you arrange this. Rates range from Rs200–250 per day for a 50–100cc scooter to double that for a more stylish 350cc Enfield Bullet.

Helmets are obligatory on national highways and in towns, and you should always carry your driving licence and the bike's insurance and registration details in case you're stopped by the police *(see page 122)*.

CLIMATE

Goa's position beside the Arabian Sea means its tropical climate sees little seasonal fluctuation in temperature, with thermometers hovering at an average maximum of between 28°C (82°F) and 32°C (90°F) for most of the year. The hottest month is usually May, during the build-up to the annual monsoons, which usually erupt in the first week of June when heavy downpours are blown in from the west.

In October, the monsoon subsides but leaves in its wake oppressive humidity. Not until the end of November does the air lose most of its moisture. From this time until around the beginning of March, the skies remain blissfully clear and the weather is perfect for the beach, with the water noticeably cooler than the air. You won't need to wear much in the evenings, or switch the fan on in your room during the night, but might need a light blanket over you in the small hours. This pleasant winter period lasts until humidity levels and temperatures start to nudge uncomfortably upwards again in early March. By the start of April, light cloud frequently turns the sky slightly hazy and the humidity can be stifling.

CLOTHING

For a beach holiday in Goa, you won't need anything thicker than the lightest cotton clothes, and perhaps a thick shawl for the occasional cool evening in December–January. Shorts and suntops or T-shirts are fine around the resorts. However, for trips into towns and markets men should wear long trousers and women keep their breasts and legs well covered in deference to local norms. And whatever you wear, make sure it's clean – most Goans wouldn't be seen dead in public with so much as a crumple in their shirt or dress.

As for footwear, flip-flops or sandals will do for strolling around the coastal resorts, but in town and inland you might be glad of a pair of trainers for excursions, especially by motorcycle. And some kind of sunhat is essential at all times of the year.

COMPLAINTS

Attitudes to efficiency differ greatly in Goa, depending on whether a business or service is run by the government (when it'll probably move at a snail's pace, if at all) or a private company (when it'll be done at lightning speed unseen elsewhere in India).

Enterprises of both types routinely offer 'Complaints' boxes, ledgers or forms for their customers. In the case of the former, submitting feedback will do little more than assuage your frustration, whereas complaining in the latter manner might actually have a tangible result. Bear in mind that complaints are always more likely to be effective if made politely, to the most senior person available.

CONSULATES

The British High Commission of Mumbai maintains a Tourist Assistance Office in Panjim – a useful contact for British nationals who've lost passports, get into trouble with the law or need help dealing with a death. It's over near the Kadamba bus stand at 13/14 Dempo Towers, Patto Plaza, tel: 243 8734, <www.ukinindia.com>.

For all other nationalities, the nearest consulate is in Mumbai: **Australia:** 16th Floor, Maker Tower 'E', Cuffe Parade (open 9am–5pm, tel: 022-2218 1071).

Canada: 41/42 Maker Chambers VI, Nariman Point (open 9am–5.30pm, tel: 022-2287 6027).

Republic of Ireland: Royal Bombay Yacht Club Chambers, Apollo Bunder (open 9.30am–1pm, tel: 022-2202 4607).

Singapore: 10th Floor, Maker Chamber IV, 222 Jamnal Bajaj Marg, Nariman Point (open 9am–noon, tel: 022-2204 3205).

South Africa: Gandhi Mansion, 20 Altamount Road (open 9am–noon, tel: 022-2389 3725).

Sri Lanka: Sri Lanka House, 34 Homi Modi Street, Fort (open 9.30–11.30am, tel: 022-2204 5861).

UK: 2nd Floor, Maker Chamber IV, Nariman Point (open 8am–11.30am, tel: 022-2283 0517).

USA: Lincoln House, 78 Bhulabhai Desai Road (open 8.30am–11am, tel: 022-2363 3611).

CRIME AND SAFETY (See also EMERGENCIES)

Only a tiny number of tourists become the victims of crime in Goa each season. Pickpocketing and muggings are extremely rare. That said, thefts from rented houses are sometimes a problem in villages such as Anjuna, Vagator and Arambol, where valuables and travel documents are best stored in secure lockers or at local banks.

In the event of any crime, particularly one for which you might later wish to file an insurance claim, go immediately to the nearest police station (your hotel will know where it is) and lodge a 'complaint' or 'incident report'. Make sure it's signed, dated and stamped, and copy the document at the first opportunity.

As with anywhere else in the world, the risk of sexual violence is a fact of life women should bear in mind when venturing out after dark, or alone in taxis. Exercise the same caution as you would at home: never walk back to your hotel late at night through quiet areas such as paddy fields, back lanes and beaches.

Before leaving home, always make a photocopy of your passport, including its identification pages and all visas, in case you lose it or it is stolen. This will make getting hold of a replacement passport much easier.

CUSTOMS AND DUTY-FREE ALLOWANCE

Currency. There is no upper limit on the amount of foreign currency visitors are permitted to bring to India, but you're not allowed to take any rupees out of the country without clearance – more trouble than it's worth unless you're in business and can employ someone to arrange the necessary paperwork on your behalf.

Duty-free allowance. Foreign tourists, other than those from neighbouring states, are permitted to import a maximum of 200 cigarettes or 50 cigars or 250g of tobacco, and one litre of wine or spirits.

E

ELECTRICITY

India operates on 220V 50Hz AC, with two- or three-round-pin plugs. Visitors from the UK, Ireland and Australia will get by with an adaptor; however, US and Canadian appliances might also need a transformer.

Electricity supplies are generally reliable in Goa these days. Power surges, on the other hand, are common, so before plugging in any sensitive electrical equipment such as a laptop computer you should consider getting hold of a current stabiliser device (or UPS, as they're known).

Indian batteries tend to run out a lot more quickly than those you're probably used to, so bring a supply from home.

EMERGENCIES

Emergency telephone numbers:
Ambulance: 102
Fire: 101
Police: 100

G

GAY AND LESBIAN TRAVELLERS

Goa, it has to be said, is a very straight destination. Same-sex relationships are not accepted among Goans themselves, and in India generally anal sex carries a 10-year prison sentence (rarely enforced, but often used by policemen to lever bribes). You'll find foreign gay and lesbian couples in the resorts, but cruising is very low-key.

Published in Mumbai, *Bombay Dost* (<www.bombaydost.com>) is a magazine that supports gay, lesbian, bisexual and transgender communities throughout India.

GETTING THERE

With the Konkan Railway up and running, and flights routed direct to Dabolim from destinations as far afield as Helsinki, getting to Goa has never been so easy. However you travel, though, it's wise to book as far in advance as possible – demand for seats during the winter season generally exceeds supply, especially over the busy Christmas–New Year holiday period.

By air (international). All direct flights to Goa from abroad are operated by charter airlines which sell seats on their planes en bloc to holiday companies, who in turn bundle them with accommodation for sale as all-in packages. It's against Indian Civil Aviation Authority (ICAA) rules to sell flights without some form of accommodation attached, but firms have been getting around this for years by stapling dummy vouchers for non-existent 'bunkhouse' rooms to the tickets. You simply ignore these as they don't entitle you to any actual accommodation.

Great Britain is the departure point for most charters to Goa, and tour operators in the UK frequently sell off seats for as low as £200 for a 15-night return (although £400 is about average). Prices rise dramatically over peak periods (ie school holidays) and with each additional week; ICAA rules also limit the maximum period a charter ticket can cover to 28 days. If you want to stay for longer than that (and many people do), you'll either have to dump the return portion of your ticket and purchase another one nearer your desired date of departure (from the travel agent Davidair on CHOGM Road, Candolim), or else go by scheduled flight. Note, too, that it is illegal to fly into India on a charter and out scheduled, and vice versa. Indian travel agents do not always tell you this when you book. Furthermore, holders of Indian passports are not allowed to purchase charter tickets.

Travelling with a scheduled airline to Goa, you'll probably be routed via Mumbai, 45 minutes' flying time north, although from southeast Asian countries and Australasia it might work out cheaper to change planes in Chennai (Madras). Your travel agent should be able to book the onward leg (with an Indian domestic carrier; see below), though you'd have to purchase tickets with web-based low-cost airlines, such as Kingfisher Airlines or Air Deccan, yourself.

By air (domestic). Seven domestic airlines operate routes to Goa from other Indian cities: Air Deccan (<www.airdeccan.net>), Air India (<www.airindia.com>), Indian Airlines (<www.indian-airlines. nic.in>), Jet Airways (<www.jetairways.com>), Kingfisher Airlines (<www.fly-kingfisher.com>), Sahara Airlines (<www.airsahara. net>) and Spicejet (<www.spicejet.com>). Ticket prices range from US$100 (Rs4,480) with swish Jet Airways, to Rs550 (US$12) or less with no-frills Air Deccan (which you can only book online or by telephone).

By train. Goa lies on the recently built Konkan Railway, connecting the state by fast express trains to Mumbai, coastal Karnataka and Kerala. However, seats are in short supply and have to be booked well in advance, or else through the premium-rate Tatkal service at a major station, such as CST/VT (Victoria Terminus) in Mumbai.

Travelling to Goa from Hampi, the main Hyderabad–Vasco line provides the quickest and most convenient approach, and costs only a fraction of what you'd pay for a taxi over the same distance.

By bus. With low-cost plane fares from Mumbai down to Rs550 or less, and the Konkan Railway fully functioning, no one travels to Goa by bus these days unless they're desperate. Both the Indian coastal highway and the main route across the Western Ghats from inland Karnataka are slow and bumpy, and the buses themselves uncomfortable.

GUIDES AND TOURS

To visit any of the places covered in this book you can either arrange one of the numerous white Maruti taxis that hang around the resorts, or else hire your own two-wheeler *(see page 109)*. Either way, independent sightseeing in Goa is a real pleasure. With your own transport you can pull over for pitstops at backcountry bars or beaches, and follow winding lanes through cashew and palm groves to encounter village life at close quarters. By travelling on a scooter or motorbike without a driver to guide you, getting lost should be considered par for the course – and half the fun. Nowhere lies much more than an hour from the coast or a major town: keep going for long enough and eventually someone will pop up to wave you in the right direction.

An alternative to independent travel are the **organised tours** you'll see advertised around the resorts. All the holiday operators and several private firms and hotels run these to destinations such as Panjim and Old Goa, Ponda and its temples, Dudhsagar Falls, the flea markets and town bazaars, as well as overnight stays in 'jungle camps' and remote beach locations; some even offer all-in trips to see the Taj Mahal in Agra. However, before signing up for one, consider the cost and compare what a taxi driver would charge for the same itinerary – you'll probably find it cheaper to book your own car for the day.

For those wishing to gain a more in-depth perspective on the local sights and culture, qualified guides may be contacted through the India Government Tourist Office – India Tourism – on Church Square in Panjim (tel: 222 3412).

The Goa Tourism Development corporation (GTDC) also organises **bus tours** to various locations. Ranging from half-day excursions to the beaches to longer trips taking in Ponda's temples, Tambdi Surla and Dudhsagar Falls, these are inexpensive but extremely rushed. Full details are posted at GTDC tourist information offices in Panjim, Mapusa and Margao, and on <www.goa-tourism.com>.

Pitched more at British charter tourists, several private firms have started to run **all-in tours** (including meals, guides and transport) to important sights, as well as much longer journeys to places such as the Taj Mahal and tiger reserves of Rajasthan. One of the largest of these is Daytripper (<www.daytrippergoa.com>), but your tour operator may also lay on such 'extension' trips, details of which will be posted at the reception in your hotel or guest house.

Various kinds of **cruises** provide other popular excursions. Around the resorts, you'll see signs advertising dolphin spotting and fishing trips, and boat rides around Goa's backwaters.

H

HEALTH AND MEDICAL CARE

The vast majority of visitors return from a trip to Goa in much better shape than they were when they left home. Even so, it's essential for travellers from outside India to seek medical advice six to eight weeks before entering the country. No vaccinations are mandatory, but some – including typhoid, hepatitis and tetanus – may be strongly recommended. In addition, some form of protection against malaria is essential, particularly during and immediately after the monsoons, when infection rates soar in towns such as Panjim, Calangute, Mapusa, Margoa and around Chaudi, near Palolem.

Apart from sunstroke, the most common ailment suffered by travellers to Goa is an upset stomach caused by contaminated food. In the worst cases, this can give rise to diarrhoea, the best treatment for which is to lay off meals for 24 hours, and to drink plenty of fluids, ideally laced with rehydration salts (available through any pharmacy). Should you pass blood or mucus, or if the diarrhoea persists for more than three or four days and is accompanied by a fever, contact a doctor. This can be done most easily through your hotel, guest house or local hosts.

Water. Is the local water safe to drink? The short answer to this is no, if the water has come out of a tap. Basically, unless it's been filtered and/or boiled, you should avoid any water that you haven't treated yourself with chlorine or iodine tablets (available from pharmacies and outdoor-sports shops in Western countries). Bottled water, which is sold everywhere in Goa, is a convenient and safe alternative, but, unfortunately, one that results in an appalling build-up of plastic litter. To minimise the impact of your holiday on the local environment, come armed with a supply of sterilising tablets and reuse your old bottles.

Hospitals. The best hospital serving north and central Goa is the **Goa Medical College** at Bambolim, 20-minutes' drive south of Panjim on the national highway (tel: 245 8700 07). In Mapusa, the **Vrindavan Hospital** has a CT scan unit (essential for dealing with head injuries). For non-life-threatening orthopaedic injuries, Dr Bale's 24-hour surgery in Porvorim (tel: 221 7709 or 221 7053), 4km (2½ miles) north of Panjim on the main Mapusa road (NH17), is also recommended. The **Apollo Victor Hospital** in Malbhat, Margao (tel: 272 8888 or 272 6272) serves south Goa, but it has less facilities than the Goa Medical College in Bambolim.

Ambulances can in theory be reached by dialling 102, but realistically you will usually get to hospital more quickly if you flag down a car or find a taxi to take you.

HOLIDAYS

The following (*overleaf*) are official public holidays in Goa. Banks and government offices close on these days, but not restaurants, shops or other private businesses. For a fuller rundown of religious and other celebrations marked in the state, *see page 95*.

December–January	*Id-ul-Fatr* (moves every year according to the lunar callendar)
26 January	Republic Day
March	*Shivratri*
March	*Holi*
March/April	Good Friday
April	*Dudi Padva*
1 May	May Day
30 May	Goa Statehood Day
June	*Milad-un-Nabi*
August	*Ganesh Chhaturthi*
15 August	Independence Day
September–October	*Dushhera*
2 October	Mahatma Gandhi's Birthday
October–November	*Diwali*
3 December	Feast of St Francis Xavier
19 December	Liberation Day
25 December	Christmas Day

L

LANGUAGE

Konkani is Goa's official language and the mother tongue of more than 90 percent of its inhabitants. India's lingua franca, Hindi (or Hindustani), is widely understood (thanks in no small part to the popularity of Bollywood films and TV soaps), but not spoken as fluently as English, the medium of the state's best educational establishments. In the towns and resorts you'll be able to get by perfectly well with English. However, if you are travelling to off-track parts of the interior a smattering of Konkani might come in useful.

Numbers. As befits a country of exceedingly large numbers, India has is own term to describe one hundred thousand – a *lakh*. One hundred million is a *crore*.

Basic Konkani phrases and numbers:

hello/goodbye	**dio boro dees diun**
yes/no	**hoee/na**
How much?	**Kitlay?**
How far is Calangute?	**Calanguti kitley pois asa?**
thank you	**dio boray lorunc**
I don't understand	**Maka naka sazmata**
My name is (David)	**Majay nau (David)**
wife	**bhai**
husband	**ghoo**
water	**oodak**
good	**borem**
May I take your photograph?	**Au eek foto kardum?**
one	**ek**
two	**dohn**
three	**teen**
four	**char**
five	**pants**
six	**soh**
seven	**saath**
eight	**aath**
nine	**nou**
ten	**dha**
twenty	**vis**
thirty	**tis**
forty	**cha-ees**
fifty	**po-nas**
one hundred	**chem-bor**
two hundred	**dho-chen**
one thousand	**ek-azar**

LAUNDRY

Virtually all hotels in Goa offer laundry *(dhobi)* services, although if you're staying in an expensive place you could save hundreds of rupees each time by taking your wash to a local 'dry cleaner' instead. 'Dry' in this case is something of a misnomer: your dirty clothes will, in fact, be taken to a laundry tank, soaked in soapy water and pounded with wooden bats until clean.

M

MAPS

From its offices and information counters, Goa Tourism sells inexpensive maps of the state featuring the road network and plans of the main towns, but they're neither detailed nor accurate enough to be good for anything more than general reference. If you aim to venture off-track and explore the interior, get hold of a copy of John Callanan's *Goa and Its Beaches* (published by Roger Lascelles), and a *Goa Town and Beach Guide*, available through most quality map outlets worldwide, or online at <www.johnthemap.co.uk>.

MEDIA

Goa has a long tradition of press freedom, with three independent broadsheet newspapers: the *Gomantak Times* (<www.gomantaktimes.com>), the *Navhind Times* (<www.navhindtimes.com>) and *O Heraldo*. All of them offer a comparable mix of regional and national news, dominated by the often dramatic vicissitudes of local government. Coverage of international events is much patchier, to say the least – to keep up with what's happening abroad, you're better off logging on to international news websites such as <www.cnn.com>, <www.guardian.co.uk> or <www.bbc.co.uk>.

TV is divided between the rather sombre government channel, Doordarshan, and the more popular satellite and cable networks, which feature lots of Bollywood action, pop music, sports, business news and

soaps. The state only has one radio station, AIR – All India Radio (also
known as *Askashvani*), broadcasting on 1287KHz AM and 105.4 FM,
but it is of limited interested to non-Goans.

MONEY

India's currency is the Rupee (Rs), divided into 100 paise. Coins come
in units of 5, 10, 25 and 50 paise, and 1, 2 and 5 rupees. Banknotes
exist in denominations of Rs5, 10, 20, 50, 100 and 500. It can sometimes be difficult to distinguish between the Rs100 and Rs500 notes,
especially in your first few days.

There exists throughout Goa, and India generally, a chronic shortage of small notes. Taxi drivers and shopkeepers, in particular, may
run out and have to send a boy to find some. When changing money,
therefore, it's a good idea to request part of the sum drawn in small
denominations.

Excessive wear and tear on the few small notes that are in circu-
lation has reduced most of them to a dreadful state. This wouldn't be
such a problem if the locals weren't so picky about the condition of
money paid to them, but the tiniest of rips will be grounds enough to
refuse a note.

Banks and Exchange. Foreign currency and travellers' cheques may
be exchanged at most banks during working hours (Mon–Fri 10am–
5pm, Sat 10am–noon). You'll be charged a percentage commission
or flat fee, but the main disadvantage with drawing money this way
is the often long wait involved for the paperwork to inch its way
through the ranks of sleepy clerks and tellers.

If you've brought Thomas Cook travellers' cheques, it's worth
going out of your way to change them free of commission at dedicated Thomas Cook offices. These can be found at 8 Alcon Chambers, Devanand Bandodkar Road, Panjim, or on the north side of
Calangute Market (both open Mon–Sat 9am–6pm, Oct–Mar also Sun
10am–5pm).

Credit and Debit Cards. Cash dispensers, or ATMs (automatic teller machines) are attached to all major banks these days (usually in air-conditioned annexes guarded by armed doormen), and these offer a fast, convenient way to withdraw money. In terms of cost, exchanging cash at an ATM may even work out cheaper than travellers' cheques: the exchange rates are usually better and the transaction charges lower (though the percentage of commission should be checked with your bank before leaving home).

The main disadvantage of relying on a credit or debit card as your main source of currency is that you'll be in a sticky situation should you lose it, or if it's swallowed by the ATM (Indian banks are obliged to return any withheld cards to their originating branch, even if it's abroad). Always carry some kind of back-up, and bring some emergency hard currency or travellers' cheques too, along with the telephone number of your bank at home should you need to contact it urgently.

O

OPENING HOURS (See also POST OFFICES)

Breakfast places open around 8am. Banks start at 10am and close at 2pm Mon–Fri, or at noon on Saturdays. Shops generally open at 10am and close and 7pm Mon–Sat. Timings vary between government offices but, as a rule of thumb, most work Mon–Fri 10am–6pm.

P

POLICE (See also EMERGENCIES)

Goa's police have earned a reputation for being among the most corrupt in the country. Some officers pay large bribes to be posted here, in the knowledge that they can recoup the outlay many times over by bribing not only the affluent locals, but also tourists (usually for minor traffic offences). If you should be stopped by the police while riding a motorcycle, simply smile and be as cooperative as possible; they'll eventually allow you to go, although you may have to pay a small bribe (of, say, Rs100) if they've caught you without a helmet, driver's licence or insurance and registration papers.

Reporting thefts of valuables or a passport is equally likely to involve bribes. For serious offences, contact your consulate *(see page 110).*

POST OFFICES

Post offices are open daily Mon–Sat 9am–8pm, and Sun 10am–5pm. Stamps can be bought from the main counters inside, but you'll have to affix them with glue (pots of revolting flour-based gloop are provided for this purpose). Air-mail letters cost Rs11, or Rs6.50 for an aerogramme and Rs6 for a postcard.

Parcels have to be wrapped in cotton, stitched and sealed in wax: the clerks will tell you where you can do this (there's usually a shop or stall near by). Unless you don't mind waiting weeks or months for your package to arrive, it's worth sending it via Speed Post. This premium service costs Rs20–60 for up to 500g inland, or Rs425–625 (up to 500g and Rs75–100 for every 250g thereafter) to foreign countries.

PUBLIC TRANSPORT

You'll doubtless be lured away from your chosen resort to visit other parts of Goa, and the transport options are many and varied.

Taxis. Around the resorts, licensed white Maruti mini-vans operated by owner-drivers take care of tourist sightseeing and trips to outlying beaches. 'Hello taxi?' will probably be the first thing you hear stepping onto the street most mornings. Fixed rates may be posted where several are attached to the same hotel, but these can usually be renegotiated, especially if you agree to use the same driver throughout your stay. Cabbies often act as informal guides and tend to regard showing their clients the best places to eat and drink as part of their job. But be warned: they also rake in commission from emporium owners, and may take you to places you never asked to visit.

At the airport and around the larger towns, taxis are painted black with yellow roofs. These tend to be older vehicles that are neither reliable nor comfortable enough for longer excursions, but they're fine for short nips across town. Fixed fares apply to and from Dabolim, but elsewhere you should settle on a rate in advance.

The same applies to the three-wheeler, black-and-yellow **auto-rickshaws** that buzz around Panjim and Margao. Again, these tend to be hard on the behind over bumpy roads, but they're great fun.

Finally, Goa is unique in India for having **motorcycle taxis**, or 'pilots'. Distinguished by their yellow mudguards, bike taxis are cheaper than autos and cars; they are also correspondingly more dangerous.

Trains. If you use the Konkan Railway at all while on holiday in Goa, it'll probably be to zip south to Gokarna, two hours from Margao. On the daily passenger service that covers this route, only one class exists. Tickets should be bought in the station prior to departure.

Buses. Travelling by bus is by far the cheapest way of getting around Goa, but at busy times the frequent stops, intense heat and general crush can be more of an ordeal than the net saving is worth. That said, buses are a good way of seeing everyday life at close quarters. Regular services start at 5.30am and run until around 9pm, connecting the resorts and main towns. Longer-distance routes are covered by the state transport company, Kadamaba, from its hub on the east side of Panjim at the end of the Mandovi road bridge.

Ferries. Flat-bottomed, diesel-powered river ferries continue to ply between village jetties in less frequented parts of the state. You'll need to jump on one to get to Terekol Fort, or across to Divar and Chorao islands from Old Goa. And Assolna, in the south, is connected to the resorts around Cavelossim by ferry. Services tend to run every 20–30 minutes; they don't operate during the night or, in the case of Kerim–Terekol, at low tide.

R

RELIGION

Around 65 percent of Goans are Hindu, with 29 percent Christian (Roman Catholic) and 5 percent Muslim. The kind of communal disharmony that occasionally afflicts the rest of India is very rare, although in 2006 riots broke out among immigrant communities in the iron-ore mining town of Sanvordem, after a mosque was demolished.

T

TELEPHONE

Privately run telephone booths are everywhere. Designated by yellow STD/ISD (Standard Trunk Dialling/International Subscriber Dialling) signboards, they're efficient and easy to use. As soon as you're connected, an electronic meter kicks in, showing you the duration and cost of the call; you pay at the end. Charges for trunk and international calls are very expensive, though drop considerably after 8pm.

Telephoning Goa from outside the state, you'll need to dial the STD prefix 0832 before the main number. From abroad, prefix 00, then the India country code, 91, then 832 (dropping the '0'), then the number.

Mobiles. Charges for mobile calls are far lower in India than most Western countries, which is why many visitors who plan to spend much time in the state sign up with a local network, such as Airtel, BPL or Idea. To do this you'll have to buy a SIM card from a mobile-phone shop; the dealer will help install it and get you connected.

TIME DIFFERENCE

Indian Standard Time is GMT plus 5½ hours, winter and summer.

TIPPING

Tipping is commonplace in hotels: a Rs10 or 20 note should be adequate for porters and room service (though in four- and five-stars, staff often expect Rs50). For good service in a restaurant or from a taxi driver, you might wish to tip 10 or 15 percent of your bill.

TOILETS

Toilets in hotels and guest houses are always Western-style **flush loos**. **Public toilets**, on the other hand, tend to be of the Asian squatting variety. At busy beachfronts and bus stations, *Sulabh Shauchalaya* complexes have been installed to reduce public defecation, but you'll find the ones in smarter restaurants more comfortable.

In Goa's coastal villages, **piggy loos** – outhouses where foraging pigs instead of running water remove the waste – are still very much the norm. Disconcerting though it is to find a bristly snout staring up at you from a hole in the floor, this method is cleaner and more environmentally friendly than conventional toilets in a region where water shortages are commonplace.

TOURIST INFORMATION

The national tourist office, **India Tourism**, has a helpful branch on Panjim's Church Square (Mon–Fri 9.30am–6pm, Sat 9.30am–1pm, tel: 222 3412). All other information counters are run by **Goa Tourism** (<www.goa-tourism.com>). They're of limited use to foreign tourists, except as a source of cheap maps, and as a means through which to arrange visits to historic *palacios* and traditional Goan houses.

V

VISAS AND ENTRY REQUIREMENTS

Visitors of all nationalities – except Nepalis and Bhutanis – need a visa to enter India. Standard multiple-entry tourist visas are valid for six months and cost £30/US$60. They're available by post from any Indian embassy, high commission or consulate.

Indian embassies and high commissions abroad include:

Australia High Commission: 3–5 Moonah Place, Yarralumla, Canberra, ACT 2600, tel: 02 6273 3999, <www.highcommissionof indiaaustralia.org>.

Canada High Commission: 10 Springfield Road, Ottawa, ON K1M 1C9, tel: 613 744 3751, <www.hciottawa.ca>.

New Zealand High Commission: 180 Molesworth Street (PO Box 4005), Wellington, tel: 04 473 6390, <www.hicomind.org.nz>.

UK High Commission: India House, Aldwych, London WC2B 4NA, tel: 020 7836 8484, <www.hcilondon.org>.

USA Embassy of India (Consular Services): 2107 Massachusetts Avenue NW, Washington DC 20008, tel: 202 939 7000.

W

WEBSITES AND INTERNET CAFÉS

The following websites provide useful information on Goa: <http://goa central.com>, <www.goa-world.com>, <www.goacom.com>, <www. goa-art.com>, <www.galeriacidade.com>, <http://goabooks.swiki.net>, <www.findall-goa.com>, <www.goanews.com>, <www.goamessenger. com>, <www.rajbhavangoa.org>, <www.goanweddings.com>.

Internet Access. Scores of small internet cafés provide access to the internet and email in Goa. An increasing number of them have faster ADSL or broadband connections, though painfully slow dial-up remains the norm outside towns and resorts. Charges are usually made per minute; slicker places sometimes charge a membership fee. Internet cafés will allow you to connect via your own laptop (for the same fee), but check they have a functioning surge protector (UPS).

WEIGHTS AND MEASURES

All but the most remote parts of India have embraced metrification for distances and weights. Two notable exceptions are jewellery and precious metals, which are weighed in old-style *tolas* – one *tola* being the weight of a British East India Company rupee: 11.66 grams.

Recommended Hotels

Most of Goa's plentiful hotel and guest-house accommodation consists of simple tiled rooms with small balconies or verandas, overhead fans and en-suite bathrooms. What you end up paying will depend on a range of factors: location (some resorts are more expensive than others), time of year (rates double or triple December–January) and proximity to the beach. Air conditioning will also bump up the tariff.

At the top end of the scale, five-star hotels maintain international standards of comfort and service. They cost significantly less than in richer countries, though you can save money by booking through a package-holiday firm, or the hotel's website. So-called 'heritage hotels' offer more interesting alternatives to the formulaic gloss of five-stars. You'll find them dotted around the state in converted colonial-era *palacios*. Taking their cue from Portuguese *pousadas*, they're furnished in traditional period style to give a taste of what Goa must have been like in centuries past.

Wherever you stay, advance booking is essential, especially over the Christmas–New Year period, when prices rise and rooms can be hard to find on spec. Reservations may be accepted over the phone, though upscale places tend to require some form of deposit.

$$$$$	over Rs3,000
$$$$	Rs2,000–3,000
$$$	Rs1,000–2,000
$$	Rs500–1,000
$	below Rs500

CENTRAL GOA

Afonso $ *St Sebastian Chapel Square, Fontainhas, Panjim, tel: 222 2359.* Handsomely restored Portuguese-era house in the heart of Panjim's most picturesque quarter, with a range of clean budget rooms and an airy rooftop terrace to lounge on in the evenings.

Casa Britona $$$$$ *Britona, near Panjim, tel: 241 0962 or 9850 557665, <www.casabritona.com>*. Set amid the mangroves 4km (2½ miles) up the Mandovi from Panjim, this compact luxury hotel combines old-world elegance (four-posters, traditional planters' chairs and a wooden deck over the water) with modern amenities such as a swimming pool and smart restaurant. The atmosphere and situation are memorable, but the rates a little ambitious.

Panjim Inn/Panjim Pousada/Panjim People's $$$ *E-212, 31 Janeiro Road, Fontainhas, Panjim, tel: 243 5628, <www.panjim inn.com>*. A trio of beautifully converted 19th-century town houses, owned and run by the same family. All three yield a vivid impression of what Goa must have felt like around the twilight of the Lusitanian empire. The decor and furniture are painstakingly in period, though the rooms are equipped with modern comforts (including air conditioning and spacious bathrooms). For pure ambience, the Pousada, a former Hindu *palacio*, has the edge on its neighbours.

NORTH GOA

Casa Sea Shell $$ *Fort Aguada/CHOGM Road, tel: 247 9879 or 277 6131, email: <Eseashellgoa@hotmail.com>*. Family-run former charter hotel that now operates independently. Opening onto small balconies on both sides, its rooms are large, impeccably clean and have good-sized bathrooms; plus you get the use of a small pool behind the building, overlooked by a chapel.

Elsewhere/Otter Creek $$$$$/$$$ *Mandrem, Pernem, tel: 253 8451 or 9820 037387, <www.aseascape.com>*. Arguably the most beautifully situated and elegantly restored period property in Goa, Elsewhere is fronted by a gorgeous pillared veranda looking across empty dunes to a stretch of undeveloped beach. You generally have to rent the house on a weekly basis: three luminous bedrooms accommodate up to six adults, or a family. Hidden from view behind it, along the banks of a tidal inlet, are a row of architectural tents called Otter Creek, offering comparable peace, seclusion and comfort. Friendly staff are on site to serve meals.

Fort Tirakol $$$$$ *Tirakol Fort Heritage, Tirakol (Terekol), Pernem, tel: 226 8258.* The views down the Pernem coast from this splendid old fort *(see page 62)* are sublime, and the ochre-washed walls and traditional Indian furniture complement the 18th-century architecture perfectly. A heritage hotel in Portuguese *pousada* style, but at more restrained rates.

Goofy's Countryside Hermitage $$$$ *Assonora, Bicholim, tel: 238 9231, email: <Egats@goatelecom.com>.* Imaginatively designed 'jungle resort' of luxury tree huts and bungalows, hidden deep in the Goan interior. Owner Godfrey Lawrence is an energetic host, leading tours to lesser-visited corners of the state. Transfers from the coast available on request.

Granpa's Inn $$$ *Gaun Waddo, Anjuna, tel: 227 3270, <www.goacom.org/hotels/granpas>.* A stylish small hotel with oodles of Goan character, on the leafy, quieter edge of Anjuna. As well as a lovely garden, the 200-year-old property has its own pool, on-site yoga school and billiards room. Popular with well-heeled alternative types that have been coming here for years.

Kerkar Retreat $$$ *Gauro Waddo, Calangute, tel: 227 6017, <www.subodhkerkar.com>.* Local artist Subodh Kerkar drew on his love of coastal colours, traditional Goan furniture and Portuguese-era architecture to transform a modern property in the thick of the charter belt into this smart little boutique hotel. It is only a short walk from the beach, and close to the main Candolim–Calangute strip.

Laguna Anjuna $$$$$ *De Mello Waddo, Anjuna, tel: 227 4305, <www.lagunaanjuna.com>.* Hip 'boutique resort' with domed laterite cottages ranged around a large free-form pool. One of Goa's trendiest addresses, and possessing much more charm and intimacy than any of the area's five-star hotels.

Leoney Resort $$$$ *Vagator, near 'Disco Valley', tel: 227 3634, <www.nivalink.com/leoneys>.* Recently built hotel comprising double-bedded chalets and larger octagonal 'cottages', all with air conditioning and terraces facing a central pool. Modern, efficient and in a peaceful corner of the village, around 15 minutes' walk from Ozran Vagator beach.

Lotus Inn $$$$ *Zor Waddo, Anjuna, tel: 227 4015, <www.lotus inngoa.com>.* Centrally air-conditioned suites and individually styled double rooms with offbeat decor pitched at well-heeled ex-hippies – in a similar mould to Laguna Anjuna, though not nearly as stylish. Its focal point is a sprawling trefoil-shaped pool overlooked by a swish Italian bar-restaurant. Set back from the shore amid the leafy fringes of Anjuna and Vagator, the location is tranquil.

Marbella $$$$ *Sinquerim, near Fort Aguada, tel: 247 9551, email: <Emarbella_goa@yahoo.com>.* One of Goa's more stylish and romantic small hotels, hidden under a giant mango tree on the hillside above Sinquerim beach (near the Taj). Its German owners have incorporated lots of old-world Goan elegance into the building's design and decor – the interiors are all beautifully furnished with traditional textiles and reproduction antiques, and most of the rooms have private verandas.

Nilaya Hermitage $$$$$ *Arpora Bhati, Arpora, tel: 227 6793, <www.nilayahermitage.com>.* Sean Connery, Kate Moss and Richard Gere number among former celebrity guests of this exclusive designer hotel, crowning a hilltop inland from Baga. Screened from hoi polloi by high walls (and even higher tariffs), its suites are all uniquely styled in vibrant Indian colours, gilded pillars and hand-crafted ironwork – the last word in alternative chic. And the view from the pool is magnificent.

Panchavatti $$$$$ *Kolo Mudi, Corjuem, near Mapusa, tel: 9822 580632.* British-Belgian expat Loulou Polak has built a palace-cum-guest house on a hilltop deep in the idyllic countryside east of Mapusa. From its enormous veranda, scattered with antique Hindu devotional sculpture and bowls of floating frangipani flowers, the grounds fall away to a huge pool and view of the distant hills. Its romantically decorated rooms, in-house masseur and fine gastronomic food are other reasons to splash out on a night or two here.

Palacete Rodrigues $$ *Near Oxford Stores, Mazal Waddo, Anjuna, tel: 227 3358.* Simple, old-fashioned guest house set in a converted late 18th-century Goan *palacio* at the heart of Anjuna, but well away from the party enclave. The fittings are a touch dowdy by modern standards, but the tariffs are correspondingly inexpensive.

Peaceland $ *Soronto Waddo, Anjuna, tel: 227 3700.* Anjuna's best-value budget place, with clean, well-aired rooms fitted with mosquito nets and backpack racks. The couple who run it are very hospitable. Set back, it's a 15-minute walk to the seafront, in one of the quieter corners of the village.

Pousada Tauma $$$$$ *Porba Waddo, Calangute, tel: 227 9061, <www.pousada-tauma.com>.* Ultra-stylish boutique hotel constructed entirely from red local laterite. The decor is low-key and the pool magical, with waterfalls and teak loungers scattered around a relaxing sun terrace, but the real selling point is a top-notch ayurvedic health spa.

Shanu $$ *Sequeria Waddo, Candolim, tel: 227 9606, email: <Eshanugoa@yahoo.com>.* Simple, well-kept rooms in a guest house whose greatest asset is its location – slap on the most peaceful stretch of Candolim beach. Reasonable tariffs, although it's quite a walk to the main strip without some form of transport.

Siolim House $$$$$ *Wadi, Siolim, tel: 227 2138, <www.siolim house.com>.* Few hotels in the state possess the heritage appeal of this magnificent 300-year-old *palacio* – former mansion of the governor of Macau. Ranged around a traditional pillared courtyard, its palatial rooms are fitted with oyster-shell windows and antique four-posters, and there's a large rectangular pool in the garden.

Villa Anjuna $$$ *Near Anjuna beachfront, Anjuna, tel: 227 3443, <www.anjunavilla.com>.* Modern, well-run hotels are a rarity in Anjuna; this one is closer to the beach than any of the competition, and has a pool and gym, but it's also only a stone's throw away from Club Paradiso's thumping sound system (the reason most of its clientele stay here).

Villa Fatima $ *Baga Road, Baga, tel: 227 7418, email: <Evilla. fatima@sympatico.ca>.* Popular backpackers' hotel in the thick of Baga's busy strip, only a short stroll across the dunes from the sea. Fifty clean, en-suite rooms (single, double and family-sized) at low rates for the area.

Villa River Cat $$–$$$ *438/1 Junasa Waddo, Mandrem, tel: 224 7928, <www.villarivercat.com>.* Sandwiched between sand dunes and a winding tidal river, this eccentric guest house, tucked away in a remote holiday enclave south of Arambol, is renowned for its hippy decor and dozens of resident cats and dogs. Convivial, comfortable and impeccably well sited, it's one of the nicest addresses this far north in the state, though the tariffs are on the high side.

SOUTH GOA

Bhakti Kutir $$$ *296 Colom, Palolem, tel: 264 3469 or 264 3472, <www.bhaktikutir.com>.* Eco-resort of ersatz tribal huts, made from natural materials and discreetly hidden under a canopy of mature palm and banana trees on the laterite headland just south of Palolem. Equipped with low-impact loos and solar-electric light, the structures are comfy and private, and all have relaxing verandas. A healthy-eating restaurant and ayurvedic healing centre are also on offer.

Coconut Creek $$$$$ *Bogmalo, near Dabolim Airport, tel: 255 6100 or 253 8100, <www.nivalink.com/coconutcreek>.* This complex of double-storeyed chalets, built with laterite and old-style terracotta-tiled roofs around a lagoon-shaped pool, ranks among south Goa's most desirable places to stay. As a base for trips further down the coast, it's a stylish and convenient option, though Bogmalo beach itself is no great shakes.

Cozy Nook $$ *Palolem beach, Canacona, tel: 264 3550.* Thai-style camp of ethnic bamboo huts at the extraordinarily scenic north end of Palolem beach, next to a tidal lagoon. The rooms are also a cut above average, with good mattresses, fans and safe lockers; plus the restaurant serves fresh, hygienic salads and other healthy food.

Dercy's $ *Agonda beach, Canacona, tel: 264 7503.* Much the most pleasant and best-value place to stay in Agonda: the accommodation is modern, en suite and tiled throughout, and equipped with quiet overhead fans; the front rooms open on to a common veranda with lovely sea views. Downstairs, a popular terrace café-restaurant is the ideal place to sample the village's stupendous grilled rockfish.

Dream Catcher $ *Palolem beach, Canacona, tel: 264 4873 or 9822 137446, email: <Elalalandjackie7@yahoo.com>.* Attractively set up hut camp which has better beds and decor than most of the other places hereabouts, and is situated right next to the river at the north end of Palolem beach. This place is a good fall-back if nearby Cozy Nook *(see page 133)* doesn't have any vacancies – and it's much cheaper.

Majorda Beach $$$$$ *Majorda, Salcete, tel: 275 4871, <www.majordabeachresort.com>.* Among the grandest in a long line of lookalike five-star resorts dotted along this vast sandy beach. Facilities include full-sized tennis courts, indoor and outdoor pools, a health spa and billiards room.

Oceanic $$ *Tembi Waddo, Colom, Palolem, tel: 264 3059, <www.hotel-oceanic.com>.* Thanks to the local municipality's ban on construction near Palolem beach, proper rooms are like gold dust in this area. Efficiently managed by a British couple, these are the most pleasantly furnished of the bunch, and benefit from a small pool and terrace restaurant to the rear of the guest house.

Park Hyatt Goa $$$$$ *Arossim beach, Salcette, tel: 272 1234, <http://goa.park.hyatt.com>.* Sprawling five-star hotel with more than 250 rooms – some with hidden gardens where you can shower al-fresco in complete privacy – built in Indo-Portuguese style. The pool is said to be Indian's biggest, and there's a glamorous spa and ayurvedic health complex, in addition to all the usual facilities you'd expect from an international-class hotel.

Simon Cottages $ *Sernabatim Ambeaxir, Benaulim, tel: 277 1839.* Most of Benaulim's accommodation consists of no-frills rooms in small guest houses, or modern tiled annexes tacked onto the side of family homes. This one's a fairly typical specimen, but larger and much better value than most in the village, with big en-suite rooms (some have kitchen space for self-catering) and welcoming owners. An ideal first stop if you've just arrived on the plane at Dabolim and are looking for somewhere inexpensive to sleep off your jet lag.

Succorina Cottages $ *1711/A Vas Waddo, Benaulim, tel: 277 0365.* A homely little guest house on the opposite, south side of the village to Simon Cottages *(see above)*, next to the fishing quarter. It's clean, welcoming and barely five minutes' walk across empty paddy fields to the beach – although it's a bicycle or scooter ride to the village shops and restaurants.

Taj Exotica $$$$$ *Cal Waddo, Benaulim, tel: 270 5666, <www. tajhotels.com>.* Along with the Park Hyatt, Goa's flagship luxury hotel: a low-rise palace set amid 22 hectares (56 acres) of lush gardens and flower-filled patios right next to the beach. The complex, whose facilities include a nine-hole golf course, ayurvedic spa, four restaurants and a kids' club, consistently gets voted 'top hotel' in the state by tour operators and business groups.

GOKARNA

Gokarna International $$–$$$ *On the main approach road to Gokarna, east of the bazaar, Karnataka, tel: 08386 256622.* Much the smartest hotel in Gokarna, with Western amenities including en-suite bathrooms and air conditioning.

HOSPET (FOR HAMPI)

Malligi Tourist Home $$–$$$$ *6/143 Jambunatha Road, off MG Road, Hospet, Karnataka, tel: 0839 428101.* This is the most comfortable base from which to explore Hampi. The rooms range from basic 'standard' options in the old block to 'de luxe' in a new wing. Both have access to a pleasant swimming pool and garden, and there are vegetarian and non-vegetarian restaurants on site.

Recommended Restaurants

Standards of cooking in Goa are extraordinarily high, and it's rare to be presented with a duff meal, even in a modest roadside fish curry-rice joint. Nor need you worry too much about hygiene. All the places reviewed here prepare their food fresh to order.

Beach shack kitchens can, admittedly, be ramshackle affairs, and few have fridges. But again, it's extremely rare to be served anything past its sell-by date. That said, it's definitely sensible to order with caution (ie avoiding meat, dairy or seafood) at places that are not busy. Hotels routinely warn guests against eating on the beaches, but shacks offer much less expensive meals and have atmosphere. After a period of experimentation, you'll soon settle on one or two favourites.

Reservations for the places listed below are recommended where a telephone number is given. Payment is nearly always made in cash; hardly anywhere accepts credit or debit cards.

$$$$$	over Rs1,000
$$$$	Rs500–1,000
$$$	Rs300–500
$$	Rs100–300
$	below Rs100

PANJIM AND CENTRAL GOA

Delhi Durbar $$$ *Mahatma Gandhi Road, behind the Hotel Mandovi, Panjim.* Offshoot of a famous Mumbai chain that's the best place in Goa to sample fine Mughlai cuisine – the north Indian style of cooking distinguished by its rich, creamy sauces and elaborate combinations of spices. Try the melt-in-the-mouth chicken *tikka*, or the delicious house speciality *rogan ghosh*.

Shiv Sagar $ *Mahatma Gandhi Road, Panjim.* The capital's slickest south Indian fast-food joint, or *udipi* (the waiters wear black ties and waistcoats), though you still have to squeeze into formica booths to eat here. The crunchy *masala dosas* (which you can order with spinach mixed into the batter), *idly-wada-sambar* and *samosas* are excellent, as is their popular Bombay-style *bhaji-pao*; and they make wonderful freshly squeezed fruit juices and *lassis*.

Viva Panjim! $$ *178 Rua 31 de Janeiro, behind Mary Immaculate High School, Fontainhas, Panjim.* Crammed into a narrow alleyway amid the colour-washed backstreets of the capital's 19th-century enclave, Fontainhas, this is the perfect spot to sample traditional Indo-Portuguese and Goan food: prawn *xacutis*, *ambot tik*, grilled kingfish *rechead* and chicken *cafreal*. Everything's fresh and carefully vetted by the lady *patronne* before it's whisked sizzling to the tables outside.

NORTH GOA

After Eight $$$ *Gauro Waddo, Calangute, near the Lifeline Pharmacy.* Swish gourmet restaurant in a candlelit garden close to St Anthony's Chapel on the main Candolim–Calangute drag. Most people come for the juicy steaks, but they also serve delicious seafood prepared in innovative Indo-Italian fusion style, plus there's plenty of choice for vegetarians. And be sure to leave room for the sublime chocolate mousse.

Amigo's $–$$ *3km (2 miles) east of Candolim at Nerul bridge, tel: 240 1123 or 9822 104920.* From its ramshackle appearance, cowering on the muddy river banks beneath Nerul bridge (which played a bit part in the 2004 Matt Damon movie, *The Bourne Supremacy*), you'd never guess this place ranked among the best seafood spots in Goa. But the fish, rustic atmosphere and prices are in a class of their own. Everything – from their house speciality, grilled snapper, to the giant crabs hauled out of the creek each night – comes straight from the family boats.

A Reverie $$$$–$$$$$ *Next to Hotel Goan Heritage, Gauro Waddo, tel: 0832/228 2597 or 9822/104512.* You won't find a more glamorous-looking place to eat than this in north Goa, and they've devised a menu that's every bit as sophisticated as the decor. From chicken breast stuffed with pistachio mousseline to mushrooms with marjoram, the dishes are all dreamed up by hostess Akriti Sinh, who works backstage while husband Virendra manages front of house. Reservations essential.

Bean Me Up $$ *Near the Petrol Pump, Chapora.* Refined wholefood cuisine that's as healthy as it is tasty. Home-made *tempeh* in cashew sauce and spicy tofu stew are the house specialities, served with steamed organic spinach and home-baked breads with dips. Plus they do a range of tempting desserts (including a yummy banana pudding with soya cream).

Blue Tao $$ *Beach Road, Anjuna.* A fantastic breakfast spot serving delicious sour-dough rye and brown breads, healthy tahini-based and nut-butter spreads, as well as herb teas and freshly squeezed juices (including wheatgrass shots).

Citrus $$$$ *Tito's Lane, Baga, tel: 9823 235465.* Classy, pure vegetarian cuisine, devised by a former animal-rescue volunteer from Birmingham in England. Drawing on worldwide influences, her recipes are all original creations, such Turkish 'meat-less' balls with smoked couscous or blue cheese and caramelised onion galettes. The wine selection is one of the best in Goa, too, and they serve proper Italian coffee.

Cuckoo Zen Garden $$$ *1.5km (1 mile) north of Candolim, off CHOGM Road.* Hidden down a winding sandy lane (signposted off the main Candolim–Calangute drag), this oriental restaurant is run by a team of enthusiastic young Taiwanese and Japanese. The cooking is painstakingly authentic, using imported and cleverly adapted local ingredients to rustle up *sushi* and other eastern delicacies. Ask for a seat on the lantern-lit rooftop.

Double Dutch $–$$ *Main Street, Arambol.* Netherlands expats Axel and Lucie threw away their passports and went into business a decade ago selling their sublime Dutch apple pie around the resorts. Their operation has since expanded into a full-blown café-restaurant up in Arambol where you can lounge under the palm canopy enjoying delights such as the famous 'mixed stuff' (stuffed mushrooms and capsicums with sesame potato), delicious cakes, pasties and biscuits, and fragrant south Indian coffee.

Fellini's $–$$ *Beachfront, Arambol*. Most of the tourist population of Arambol converges on this Italian-run restaurant each evening for its wonderful pasta dishes, pizzas and gnocchi, served with a choice of over 20 different sauces at backpacker-friendly prices.

Fiesta $$$$ *Tito's Lane, Baga, tel: 227 9894*. Twinkling with fairy lights and lanterns, Fiesta has been Baga's most extravagantly dressed (and highly rated) restaurant since its glamorous owners came here from Mumbai. The Mediterranean-Portuguese menu has stood the test of time: house specialities include buffalo mozzarella salad, clam paella and juicy wood-baked pizzas.

Florentine's $$ *Saligao, 4km (2½ miles) inland from Calangute, next door to the Ayurvedic Natural Health Centre (ANHC)*. The reputation of this no-frills Goan eatery at Saligao, a short drive inland from Calangute, rests on just one dish: Mrs D'Costa's famous chicken *cafreal*. Chefs from the Taj have even been known to sneak in to sample the flavour-packed curry, and the prices are as down to earth as the ambience. An absolute must.

F.R. Xavier's $–$$ *Municipal Market complex, Mapusa*. The perfect pit stop if you've worked up an appetite shopping in Mapusa's Friday market. F.R. Xavier's has done a roaring trade with the local middle classes for decades, and its style and menu have changed little since the 1930s. The veg and beef flaky pastry 'patties', prawn curry and Goan-style *samosas* are all delicious, but the old-world atmosphere is the main appeal here.

Infantaria Pastelaria $–$$ *Next to St John's Chapel, Baga*. A sub-venture of the famous Souza Lobo restaurant on the seafront *(see page 141)*, Calangute's busiest bakery pulls in streams of locals and tourists for its croissants, apple pies and traditional Goan sweets and cakes (including *dodol* and *bebinca*). You can eat under paddle fans on the open-sided ground-floor terrace, or on the first floor, where they serve main meals in the evenings.

J&A's $$$$–$$$$$ *Baga Creek, Baga, tel: 227 5274, <www. littleitalygoa.com>.* One of Goa's unmissable gastronomic experiences: an Italian restaurant serving beautifully presented, scrupulously authentic dishes alfresco in front of an old fisherman's cottage beside Baga Creek. Start with carpaccio of beef or an innovative green salad, and take time over their whopping steaks or a seafood lasagne (leaving room for the lemon cheesecake).

Lila Café $$–$$$ *Baga Creek, Baga.* Five minutes' walk up Baga Creek from the box bridge, this German-run bakery-café is a relaxing place for breakfast or to escape the midday heat. Lounging on low-slung bamboo chairs, you can peruse the papers over fresh coffee and healthy snacks such as aubergine pâté or buffalo 'ham' with Nilgiri cheese and home-baked wholemeal bread.

Pete's Shack $$ *Escrivao Waddo, Candolim.* Beach cafés tend to have their ups and downs, but this one, near Shanu's guest house at the north end of Candolim beach, has been steadily improving for years. Choose from their ever-expanding repertoire of hygienic salads, dressed with real olive oil and balsamic vinegar, or mains of seafood sizzlers and tandoori specialities. For dessert, they also do a knockout chocolate mousse.

Plantain Leaf $–$$ *Market area, Calangute.* Housed in a grand laterite dining hall with marble tables, this top-notch, strictly vegetarian *udipi* serves the standard range of spicy south India fast food – *dosas*, *idlys*, *wadas*, *samosas* and *uttapams* – in addition to good-value *thalis* and an exhaustive north Indian menu.

Sea Shell $$ *Fort Aguada Road, Candolim.* Popular multi-cuisine restaurant, spread across the terrace of a stately 19th-century Goan *palacio* on Candolim's main strip. It caters mainly for British charter tourists, with copious sizzlers, steaks and fresh seafood, as well as a full range of Chinese and Indian. Genuinely hospitable and very good value for money.

Sheetal $$ *Murrod Waddo, Candolim.* The best place in north Goa for quality Mughlai cuisine. Served in shiny copper *karais* on charcoal braziers, the chicken, mutton and vegetable dishes bubble in creamy concoctions that will put your local Bangladeshi take away in the shade. If hot spices aren't really your thing, try the milder *murg malai* – chicken in delicious cashew-nut sauce.

Souza Lobo $$ *On the beachfront, Umta Waddo, Calangute, tel: 228 1234, <www.souzalobo.com>.* Stuffed crab, baked kingfish and seafood 'crêpe Souza' are the specialities of this near-legendary restaurant on Calangute beachfront. It was here long before the advent of foreign tourism, catering for Mapusa and Panjim's middle classes. Sadly, however, it has somewhat fallen off the pace in recent years and no longer deserves the reputation it once enjoyed, though the old-fashioned atmosphere and location are worth at least one visit.

Stone House $$ *Fort Aguada/CHOGM Road, Candolim, tel: 247 9909.* Groaning portions of beef steak and kingfish fillets, accompanied by baked potatoes, are the trademarks of this lively restaurant in south Candolim. Laid out on a terrace in front of the eponymous stone house, it has a great location and loads of atmosphere, staying open late most nights, when owner Chris D'Souza cranks up his beloved blues music at the bar.

SOUTH GOA

Cozy Nook $$ *Palolem Beach, Canacona, tel: 264 3550.* Salads are generally to be avoided in India, but you can enjoy them in perfect safety at this hip little beachside restaurant, situated on the north side of Palolem next to the tidal creek. Every lunchtime, they lay on an 'eat-as-much-as-you-like' buffet, prepared fresh with leaves and vegetables that have been washed thoroughly in chlorinated water.

Dercy's $$ *Agonda beach, Canacona, tel: 264 7503.* It's worth travelling down to Agonda just to eat at Dercy's, a small family-run place set back from the beach, where there's generally only one thing on the menu: local rockfish. Steeped in heavenly garlic butter, portions are huge and the chips cooked to perfection.

Droopadi $$–$$$ *Palolem beach, Canacona*. Sophisticated north Indian dishes prepared by a top-class Mughlai chef slap on the beach. The *tandoori* fish, chicken *tikka masala* and lamb kebabs are mouth-watering, and the creamy curries, laced with saffron and dry-roasted almonds, sublime when scooped up with a naan bread crisp from the oven.

Durigo's $–$$ *Sernabatim, north of Maria Hall crossroads, Ben aulim*. Rough-and-ready locals' fish restaurant where you can sample real Goan-style seafood for a fraction of the price at Martin's Corner *(see below)*. Order at least one plate of mussels *(shenanio)*, lemonfish *(modso)* and barramundi *(chonok)*, either smothered in fiery red *rechead* paste or pan-fried in crunchy *rawa* millet.

Longuinho's $$ *Luis Miranda Road, Margao*. An old-style café that's been a Margao institution since colonial times. It recently had a much needed make-over, but the snack menu of beef, prawn and veg patties hasn't altered for decades. A good place to cool off after shopping in the market.

Martin's Corner $$$ *Betalbatim, tel: 288 061*. Mrs Martin, who started out rustling up rice and chilli fry for local cabbies, is regarded as a High Priestess of Goan cuisine. Crammed every night with big-spending foreigners from the nearby luxury resorts, the restaurant has come a long way since its humble beginnings. But Mrs M remains at the helm, personally overseeing the preparation of her famous *masalas*. The menu is vast, but stick to the Goan favourites such as chicken *cafreal*, fish *caldin*, *xacuti*, pomfret *rechead* or lobster in butter-garlic sauce. Reservations highly recommended.

Oriental $$$$ *Murrod Waddo, tel: 309 2809*. Wonderful Thai cuisine, prepared and presented in great style by Master Chef Chawee. A choice of 18 house sauces accompany prime cuts of seafood, meat and poultry, and there are plenty of vegetarian options. You must try their amazing papaya salad starter.

INDEX